GW01035554

B-24 Liberator Groups

Of the 8th Air Force

IN FOCUS

RED
KITE

**This volume is dedicated to my great friend,
Colonel Carl J. Gjelhaug of Riverside, California,
who as a very young man received his baptism of fire at the
controls of the B-24 Liberator**

All rights reserved.
No part of this publication may be
reproduced, stored in any form of
retrieval system, or transmitted in any
form or by any means without prior
permission in writing from the
publishers.

First published 2007 by
Red Kite
PO Box 223
Walton on Thames
Surrey, KT12 3YQ

www.redkitebooks.co.uk

© 2007 Mike Bailey

Printed by Cromwell Press,
Wiltshire.

ISBN 9780954620196
B-24 Liberator Groups
of the 8th Air Force

Designed by
Simon W Parry

Contents

Acknowledgements

The photographs contained within these pages have been collected over a period of some forty-odd years and have been contributed by official organisations and private individuals, many of whom served with the Bomb Groups featured in this volume. As the same photo was sometimes sent by more than one person I will list contributors below rather than with the captions.
Many thanks to the following:
Steve Adams, John Archer, Allan G Blue, Martin Bowman, Fred Breuninger, Bob Coleman, Gerry Collins, Pat Everson, Roger A Freeman, Charles Freudenthal, William Green, Carl J Gjelhaug, Ursel P Harvell, Ian Hawkins, Herman Hetzel, James Hoseason, Tony Kerrison, Barry Ketley, Jim Kiernan, Sharon D Kiernan, Ian Maclachlan, Wily Noble, Tony North, Pat Ramm, Rick Rokicki, George Reynolds, Darin Scorza, Brendon Wood, 2nd Air Division Association US Air Force, Swiss Air Force.

Front Cover:
'Arise My Love and Come with Me' B-24 J-5-FO (42-50768) of the 754th Squadron, 458th Bomb Group. The photograph was taken at Horsham St Faith in the summer of 1944 with the crew of Howard Stanton posing in front, but this crew did not fly this particular B-24 operationally.

Title Page:
'Mah Akin Back' B-24 J-150-CO (44-40226) T8-F of the 491st Bomb Group at rest at Metfield during the summer of 1944 was one of those Liberators to survive the European war.

Previous Page:
With engines thundering at full power 'Final Approach' commences its take-off roll at Horsham St Faith late in the war. 'Final Approach' (B-24 H-15-FO 42-52457) of the 752nd BS, 458 BG completed no less than 122 missions before she was shot down over Lechfeld on 9th April 1945.

The B-24 Liberator

In the year of 1938, with war clouds gathering over Europe and Asia and the future political situation looking anything but optimistic the government of the United States began taking realistic consideration of its defence capabilities. The Boeing Aircraft Company in Seattle, Washington State, was producing early models of its B-17 Flying Fortress heavy bomber for the US Army Air Corps at this time. The first Fortress took to the air back in 1935 and it was proving to be a reliable and sturdy aircraft. However, with the deteriorating political situation it appeared likely that the United States could be needing many more of these bombers in the not too distant future. If production of the B-17 was to be significantly increased, there would be a need for an additional source of output. With the above needs in mind the US Army Air Corps approached the Consolidated Aircraft Corporation of San Diego , California, with a proposal to gear-up for the production of the Boeing bomber. Prior to this the Consolidated company had gained quite a reputation as a producer of good, reliable, flying boats such as the PBY Catalina.

The President of Consolidated (CAC) Major Reuben H Fleet, called together his board of directors to consider the Amy's proposals and then had a close and lengthy discussion with his chief designer, the very capable Isaac M Laddon. They very soon came to the conclusion that their company could conceive and produce a heavy bomber of a more modern and superior design than the B-17, all within the timescale it would take them to gear-up and organise for full scale B-17 production. Not a moment was lost and within a very short time Isaac Laddon and his design team came up with a set of plans and then a mock-up of the proposed new bomber. The Army experts were impressed and gave the go-ahead to produce a prototype, and contracts were signed on 30th March 1939.

Consolidated then went flat-out to produce the prototype and in record time the gleaming silver Model 32, or XB-24, was rolled out into the California sunshine. With chief test pilot William B Wheatley at the controls she took to the air for her maiden flight on 29th December 1939. On that day little did anybody at Consolidated realise that this prototype would be the first of over 18,000 Liberators to follow over the next five-to-six years; a record production run for any bomber aircraft and eventually needing five production facilities to cope with the huge demand.

The usual teething troubles found in every new design were gradually tackled and cured. It was very soon realised that Consolidated had a very dependable aircraft to equip the Army Air Corps with. Even before America's entry into World War II the RAF were using initial production models on its return ferry service across the vast reaches of the North Atlantic, a task ideally suited to the Consolidated aircraft due to its tremendous range capabilities. This endurance so impressed the British that very early production machines were modified as anti U-Boat patrol bombers for RAF Coastal Command squadrons which were soon covering formerly unreachable areas of the North Atlantic with great success.

With production well underway the design was gradually perfected month-by-month, modified and up-dated. With America's entry into the war manufacture went into overdrive and with additional production centres turned over to construction, variations in Liberator type were soon in evidence. The basic design

The very first Liberator. The XB-24 took to the air for its maiden flight on 29th December 1939, with William B Wheatley at the controls. The XB-24 is seen here sometime later, taxiing out for a test flight and fitted with updated turbosupercharged engines.

was so successful that it was found suitable for conversion to many roles including transport, anti-submarine patrol bomber, tanker etc. as well as its primary role as a strategic bomber.

America found itself embroiled in a long distance war in the Pacific and as improved bomber versions of the B-24 came into service these were found much more suitable to cope with the vast distances than was the B-17, so Liberators gradually replaced the Fortress in that theatre of war. However, the very first bombing mission carried out by a Liberator took place on the night of 10-11th January 1942, when a Liberator II of No.108 Squadron RAF took off from Fayid in Egypt to bomb Tripoli Harbour.

As the war progressed the B-24 found itself operating in all theatres of war ranging from the Aleutians in the north to Australia in the south. In 1944 when Britain turned on to the offensive in South East Asia the Liberator really came into its own as a long range bomber with several RAF squadrons operating from the Indian sub-continent. Its long range capability made it the ideal weapon to carry the war to the Japanese. Many of the targets in Burma, Thailand and Malaysia were at prodigious distances and the RAF squadrons started a programme to increase range even further and experiments with power settings, mixture control and fuel balancing were carried out with results that even surprised representatives from the manufacturers.

Above: **One of only nine B-24cs built cruises over San Diego Bay with the Consolidated factory and Lindberg Field in the background. The B-24C was used to prove the modifications installed in the following B-24D including turbo-chargers, top and rear turrets, etc. This photo was taken at about the time of America's entry into World War II.**

Back in Europe, with Italy gradually being secured by the Allies, the Liberator and Fortress bases as well as RAF B-24 airfields were established and soon the vast 15th Air Force was hitting targets in the Balkans, Austria and Southern Germany. Whilst this was taking place, back in England the Liberator was really making its presence felt with the Eighth Air Force, and new Bomb Groups were constantly being added to the huge armada of heavy bombers building up in eastern England.

The B-24 was an ingenious concept which incorporated some radical new innovations in its design; one of which was the high aspect ratio, low-drag, high-lift wing which gave the 'Lib' a span of 110 feet. This wing was fitted with the Fowler flaps which considerably assisted controlled landing speeds. The very graceful and efficient airfoil designed by David R Davis had previously been tried and tested on the Consolidated Model 31 flying boat. Most unusual for an aircraft of its size, the main landing gear retracted outwards and upwards into the wing itself, a radical departure from the usual method of retraction into the underside of the inner engine nacelles. The design enhanced performance by the further reduction of drag and also left the underside of the nacelle free to incorporate the exhausts for the turbo-superchargers which were introduced to the 'Lib' as production moved forward.

The 'Lib' was also the first heavy bomber to use the nose wheel landing gear which eased ground handling and made take-offs and landings that bit easier. Further streamlining was effected by the design of the bomb doors which, instead of opening out into the airstream in the

conventional way, causing drag and buffeting, actually slid in groves upwards around the contours of the fuselage. Although an advantage in many ways, the flexibility of the doors made water landings extremely hazardous and one didn't ditch a B-24 unless it was absolutely unavoidable.

The Liberator was fitted with four excellent and very reliable Pratt-Whitney R1830 engines which produced 1200hp each and in the B-24 C and D onward these engines were updated with turbo-superchargers which gave a much improved performance at high altitude. Another design feature borrowed from the Model 31 flying boat was the 12 foot high vertical stabilisers and rudders.

Throughout its evolution each production batch was gradually updated with the latest technical developments such as improved armament, navigation and radio aids and blind bombing equipment. The result was that the late versions of B-24s outwardly barely resembled the early models.

The Eighth Air Force commenced B-24 operations with the 93rd BOMB GROUP in October 1942 and gradually increased its strength until the summer of 1944 when no less than nineteen Liberator groups were operating in the purely strategic bombing role whilst other units engaged in various other activities such as radio-countermeasures and clandestine operations.

The vast majority of Liberator groups were concentrated in the Second Air Division, whilst five operated alongside the B-17 groups in the Third Air Division. The First Division comprised all Fortress groups.

The Third Division experienced some problems in operating both types together as their respective performances were not really compatible. Although the B-24 enjoyed a slightly higher combat cruise speed advantage over the B-17, this was negated when trying to keep in-step with the Fortress formations. Also, the Fortress handled better at extreme altitude, whereas the 'Lib' became rather unstable and difficult to handle when fully loaded and in tight formation at these heights. The Liberator was much happier flying in formation a few thousand feet lower. This performance incompatibility led the Eighth's boss, Lieutenant General Jimmy Doolittle, to standardise on the B-17 in the Third Division and their 'Lib' groups converted on to the B-17 whilst most of their B-24s were transferred to the Second Air Division.

The original Eighth Air Force groups, the 93rd, 44th and 389th, were initially equipped with the B-24D. This was a good model, but combat experience proved it somewhat lacking in forward defensive armament as its streamlined, framed plexiglass nose was equipped with three hand-held 0.5 Browning machineguns which were difficult to manipulate in the cramped confines.

In the late summer of 1943 new groups began arriving from the USA equipped with the latest H and J model Liberators fitted with power operated turrets designed to counter enemy head-on attacks. Whilst this very necessary new innovation tended to spoil the aerodynamic shape of the nose section and also mar the forward view for the navigator and bombardier, the extra weight of the new tur-

Above: **Over three years after the previous photo was taken B-24 M-20-FO is captured on a test flight over Michigan; the 8,000th Lib to be built by Ford. The B-24 M-20-FO was the last version to be issued to the Eighth Air Force.**

ret altered the centre of gravity and actually improved the aircraft's flight attitude or 'sit' which had previously been rather nose-up.

Like some of the final production Ds these new Hs and Js were all equipped with a ventral two-gun turret beneath the mid fuselage. This ball turret could be lowered and raised at will.

The most significant variation between the H and J models was the automatic pilot and bombsight. The H model carried the Sperry S-1 sight and the A-5 autopilot; whilst the J model had the Norden M-9 sight and the C-1 autopilot. This could cause frustration with bombardiers who were trained on the Norden sight, only to find themselves assigned to B-24Hs upon arrival in England. This led to high pressure 'cramming' on the unfamiliar Sperry sight. In the Eighth Air Force this Sperry sight was confined to the H model only, with subsequent models reverting back to the Norden.

By 1944 no less than five production plants were churning out B-24s at speed. In an effort to identify Liberators from these various sources each manufacturing facility was given a two letter code as follows:

CO Consolidated, San Diego, California
CF Consolidated, Fort Worth, Texas
DT Douglas, Tulsa, Oklahoma
NT North American, Dallas, Texas
FO Ford, Willow Run, Michigan

It might be imagined that each of these plants would be producing Liberators identical in every way to each other, but this was far from the case. Examples of the same model of, say, a B-24J could differ in detail according to the place of manufacture and this aspect of 'Liberator Lore' has been clarified in the photo captions throughout this book.

The majority of Liberators which were destined for the Eighth Air Force were H and J models, whilst the G version mostly went to the Fifteenth Air Force in Italy. The most numerous version of the B-24 was the J, which varied in itself enormously depending on time and place of manufacture. The J was superseded on the San Diego production lines in late 1944 by the L, although only the Ford produced L reached the Eighth Air Force. The standard tail turret of Ls reaching England was replaced by a new special light-weight cupola with two hand-held 0.5 machineguns. This very neat innovation saved quite an amount of weight and also slightly reduced fuselage length. Most of these Ls were converted into H2X Radar or 'Mickey Ships' as they were called, with the Radar scanner housed in the position formerly occupied by the ball turret. This conversion had previously taken place on various H and Js. Most ball turrets had been removed from Liberators in the Summer of 1944.

The ultimate version to see service with the Eighth Air Force was the M. This was similar to the L, but reverted to the conventional tail turret. As in the final L versions the M built by Ford had improved, elongated scanning windows each side of the nose section. This was an attempt to aid the navigator who's view from the nose in turret versions had always been restricted. Bulged side windows on the flight deck were also installed and in the final M batches, a few of which reached the Second Air Division before hostilities ended, an entirely re-worked cockpit canopy was incorporated. This had a V shaped windscreen, a reduction of framing and pull-down escape panels above the pilot and co-pilot's head.

All the Eighth Air Force's Ms were the Ford model, except for a handful of San Diego versions which were modified to carry a new type of Radar scanner in the shape of a small additional wing. This was known as 'Eagle' and its housing was attached to the lower fuselage just ahead of the forward bomb bay. These were operated by the 482nd Bomb Group, a specialized Radar Pathfinder unit that operated both the B-17 and B-24.

Below: **Among the first of many to come. Seen here at Alconbury in late 1942 'Katy Bug' is a very early example of the B-24D and belonged to the 93rd BG, the first Liberator group in the UK. Note the complete lack of unit markings on the original planes. Very soon an individual radio call letter would be added to the vertical fin. This atmospheric shot shows to advantage the 110 foot span of the graceful Davis wing.**

44th

BOMB GROUP

44th Bombardment Group (H)

Component Squadrons

Squadron	Code
66th Sqn	QK
67th Sqn	NB
68th Sqn	WQ
506th Sqn	GJ

Operational bases:
Shipdam, Norfolk, (plus detachments to Benina-main, Libya and Oudna, Tunisia, 1943)

First mission
7th November 1942
Last mission
25th April 1945

Total Combat Missions
343 missions

Group Markings
No distinctive group markings carried until return from the first detachment to North Africa at the end of August 1943. From then on they carried a white disc containing a dark blue, sometimes black, A on the outer vertical tails and upper right wing. From late May 1944 vertical tails were white with a black vertical band.

Right and below: **When the 44th and 93rd BGs commenced operations in late 1942 no group or squadron identification markings were carried, apart from the aircraft's call letter on the vertical tail surface. Seen here**

Above: **The earliest Liberator operated by the 44th BG was the 66th Squadron's 'SNAFU' B-24 D-CO (40-2354). She is seen here at Bovingdon in September 1942 whilst undergoing armament evaluation. Just visible is the non-standard gun mounting below the fuselage just aft of the bomb bay. 'SNAFU' was lost a year later on 16 September 1943 in a mid-air collision off Selsey, Sussex. She was the twelfth D off the production line.**

practicing low-level formation flying over Attleborough prior to depature to North Africa for the Ploesti oil refinery mission is B-24 D-25-CO (41-24225) from the 68th Squadron. She soon aquired the name 'Flak Alley' with accompanying risqué artwork on both sides of her nose. She was lost on her 42nd mission, to Gotha on 24th February 1944.

Above: **The first B-24Hs sporting nose turrets began arriving in the autumn of 1943. This pleasing study shows Ford built B-24 H-1-FO (42-7549) banking over the Norfolk farmlands at Wayland near Attleborough. Note the very large national insignia on the very early Ford built Hs. The white tail disc with dark blue letter was used from September 1943.**

Inset: **A portrait of the same plane, displaying the name 'Moby Dick' beneath its Emerson nose turret. Also of interest is the mounting for the Sperry bombsight and flexible hot air tube for both bombsight and optical glass sighting panel. 'K' crash landed at Woodchurch, Kent, on 16th March, 1944 and was written off.**

Right: **British Foreign Secretary, Mr Anthony Eden addressing the 44th BG during a goodwill visit to Shipdham, June 25th, 1943. At attention behind is Captain Robert E Miller (far left) and his combat crew, whilst Lieutenant General Jacob L Devers is to Mr Eden's left. The B-24 is 'Fascinatin Witch' B-24D (41-23811) 'K' of the 66th BS. This photo shows to advantage the gun arrangement in the nose of a B-24D. The 'Witch' was lost on 1st October 1943 on a mission to Wiener Neustadt, Austria.**

Above: **Two views of 'Sack Artists' from the 67th BS. She was an early Consolidated San Diego built B-24 J-65-CO (42-100073). This version differed considerably from the Ford built H. She carried the Consolidated A-6-A nose turret; basically the standard tail turret with faired-in frontal area, inward opening nose wheel doors, differently moulded bombardier's transparency and braced pitot tubes. She was lost on 18th March 1944 on a Friedrichshafen mission.**

Below: **New unpainted Liberators began arriving in April and May 1944 and as the white tail disc with blue letter didn't stand out well against the silver aluminium, it was decided to use a dark blue disc with a white letter. This was very soon changed when new all painted vertical tails appeared in late May. An example of the interim tail markings is seen here on B-24 H-25-FO (42-9508) of the 67th BS. She had a long and distinguished career and survived hostilities to return to the USA after completing 120 missions.**

Above: **A picture that is charged with dramatic atmosphere. Ambulances and crash trucks stand by as the 506th BS slowly taxi around Shipdham's perimeter track for take-off. The peace of the Norfolk countryside is shattered by the roaring of scores of Pratt & Whitney engines and the squealing of brakes.**

Below: **During the final days of the European air war these 506th BS 'Libs' pass over the North Norfolk coast; Holkham Hall in its parkland can be discerned in the lower right corner of this photo.**
Nearest aircraft is the pristine new B-24 M-10-FO (44-50748) 'Big Headed Kid' at lower left is 'Clean Sweep' a B-24 J-5-DT (42-51351).

The **44th Bomb Group** selected B-24 D-1-CO (41-23699) as their assembly ship. She was over painted with yellow and black stripes, but retained her mission scoreboard and her 'Flying Eightball' symbol.
During her career her paint scheme was revised to change from the early disc on the tails to the later white tail with black vertical stripe.
She was originally named 'Lemon Drop' and retained the painting of a lemon on her starboard nose.

93rd

BOMB GROUP

93rd Bombardment Group (H)

Component Squadrons

Squadron	Code
328th Sqn	GO
329th Sqn	RE
330th Sqn	AG
409th Sqn	YM

Operational bases
Alconbury, Huntingdonshire; Hardwick, Norfolk; plus detachments to Tarfaraoui, Algeria; Gambut Main, Libya; Benghazi, Libya; and Oudna, Tunisia, 1943.

First mission
9th October 1942
Last mission
25th April 1945

Total Combat Missions
396 missions

Group Markings
No distinctive group markings carried until return from the first detachment to North Africa at the end of August 1943. From then on they carried a white disc containing a dark blue, sometimes black, B on the outer vertical tails and upper right wing. From late May 1944 vertical tails were painted deep yellow with a black vertical band.
Many 330th Squadron planes carried a distinctive whale mouth and later in the war 409th Squadron aircraft carried yellow cowl rings and prop domes. Pathfinder B-24s in the 329th Squadron had their noses painted red, whilst Pathfinders in the 328th Squadron sported yellow and black chequerboard noses.

Above: **Shortly after arrival in England and initially based at Alconbury, Huntingdonshire, before moving to Hardwick, Norfolk. 'Eager Beaver' rests at ease on her hardstand whilst ordnance crews fit nose and tail fuses to 1,000 pound bombs.**
'Eager Beaver' (41-23737) was a B-24 D-1-CO model and was eventually taken over by the 446th BG where she was painted overall in international orange, re-named 'Fearless Freddy' and used as the group's assembly ship.
Early B-24Ds featured needle bladed propellers, which were replaced by wider 'paddle blades' a little later in the production run. The photos show the original nose armament of three 0.5 Colt-Browning hand-held machineguns. In many cases the front gun was raised higher up the bombardier's transparency and linked with an additional gun, but the navigator and bombardier had great difficulty in manipulating these heavy weapons in the teeth of a 200mph airstream and in the face of a determined head-on assault.

Right: **'Katy Bug' was B-24 D-1-CO (41-23745) which was written off in a crash landing at Alconbury on 18th November 1942.**

15

Left: Pleasing formation shot of 'Joisey Bounce' (41-24226 'L' of the 330th BS) with 'Duchess' (41-24147) and 'Boomerang' (41-23722 'C' of the 328th BS).

Below: 'On The Ball' (42-40990) from the 328th Squadron. In an attempt to improve nose defence, in some cases an extra weapon was linked with the existing gun in the bombardier's panel and repositioned slightly higher up the panel for better elevation. This arrangement is evident here.

Below: A typical Liberator crew during the early days of Eighth Air Force operations. Whilst the officers (pilot, co-pilot, navigator and bombardier) are wearing A2 jackets, the enlisted crew members are clothed in the rather heavy and cumbersome leather fleece-lined suits which were later replaced by more efficient and lighter heated garments.
The aircraft is 'Flying Cock' B-24 D-1-CO (41-23724) of the 409th BS.

Above: **B-24 J-55-CO (42-99949) 'Naughty Nan' displaying her newly applied 328th Squadron letters. Nose and top turrets are traversing to the 2 o'clock high sighting position. Ball turret is retracted, but ready to enter with guns pointing downwards. The small projection below the A-6-A nose turret is just another B-24 in the distance.**

'Naughty Nan' was a very curvaceous blonde, painted in the right side of the nose. She was lost on 21st September 1944 when she collided in mid-air with another B-24 and crashed near Ingelmunster, Belgium.

Left: **From the late summer of 1944 pathfinder aircraft in the 329th Squadron had their noses painted bright red. One example was 'Lucky Lass' B-24 J-150-CO (44-40157). This lass originally flew with the ill-fated 492nd BG and survived hostilities.**

Left: The Liberator could look graceful from some angles. Here 'Lindie' peels away from the formation to enter the landing pattern. She was a B-24 H-25-FO (42-95043) and crashed into the sea off Eastchurch, Kent, on return from a mission on 4th August 1944.

Right: Displaying her whale mouth 'Sweet Chariot' of the 330th BS was a Ford built B-24 J-5-FO (42-50829). She ditched 37 miles off Orfordness, Suffolk, on return from an airborne army supply drop on 18th September 1944.

Left: Back in the USA a Liberator at a training base was elaborately decorated with a yellow head and dripping red mouth, resembling a tiger. A coloured photo of this appeared in a US aviation publication that was distributed to the Eighth Air Force bases in England. This idea caught on with many of the combat crews and very soon most groups had their own version. The 93rd's example is seen here on her hardstand at Hardwick. She was B-24 J-5-DT (42-51359) of the 329th Squadron. She survived to return to the USA.

Right: **The veteran 'Ball of Fire' B-24 D-1-C) (41-23667) was 'Judas Goat' at Hardwick, home of the 93rd Bomb Group. She was originally painted with yellow, white and natural olive-drab.**

Below: **Later her olive-drab stripes were over painted in red. Finally the yellow was over painted in white as seen here. Where the yellow was changed to white it left a bluish grey, off white effect.**

Above: **'Ball of Fire' over the village of Hempnal, Norfolk.**

Below and right: **'Ball of Fire' was later replaced by B-24 D-165-CO (42-72869), formerly 'Bear Down', and painted with wide yellow bands around her nose and rear fuselage.**

389th BOMB GROUP

389th Bombardment Group (H)

Component Squadrons

Squadron	Code
564th Sqn	YO
565th Sqn	EE
566th Sqn	RR
567th Sqn	HP

Operational bases:
Hethel, Norfolk; plus detachments to Benghazi, Libya; and Massicault, Tunisia, 1943.

First mission
9th July 1943
Last mission
25th April 1945

Total Combat Missions
321 missions

Group Markings
No distinctive group markings carried until return from the first detachment to North Africa at the end of August 1943. From then on they carried a white disc containing a dark blue, sometimes black, C on the outer vertical tails and upper right wing. From late May 1944 vertical tails were painted black with a white vertical band.

Above: **'Missouri Mauler'** A B-24 D-20-CF of the 567th BS climbing to altitude. She carried a kicking Missouri mule on her nose. This batch of B-24 Ds did not carry a ball turret, but had a single hand-held 0.5 Browning in the rear underside hatch, just visible below the left vertical stabilizer. Like 'Screamin Mimi' she was later assigned to the 801st BG (P).

Above right: **'Screamin Mimi'** and companions in flight in the summer of 1943. She was a B-24 D-120-CO (42-40997) and later went on to serve with the clandestine 801st BG (P) on night operations.

Right: **Novel nose art on 'Screamin Mimi' after nine operations.**

Above: The view from the right waist window early in 1944 of 'Jackass Male' (B-24 D-165-CO, 42-72866) of the 565th Squadron and 'Galloping Katie' (B-24 J-90-CO, 42-100332) from the 566th Bomb Squadron. On 16th March 1944 'Galloping Katie' was badly damaged and landed at Dubendorf, Switzerland, where she and her crew were interned.

Below: Undergoing engine maintenance on her hardstand at Hethel in the early spring of 1944 is a veteran B-24D. It has recently had the 'HP' code letters applied and the protective boiler plate bolted to the fuselage beneath the cockpit side windows shows 51 mission symbols including the Ploesti raid. By this time the needle propeller blades had given way to paddle blades. This was B-24 D-95-CO (42-40743) that became the assembly ship for the 492nd BG and was decorated with white stripes.

Above: **High above the continent of Europe is B-24 J-75-CO (42-100146) from the 564th BS. She later moved to the 567th BS and adopted the name 'Mistah Chick' with the call leter U+. She ended her war in a crash landing at Halmstad, Sweden, on 20th June 1944.**

Below: **A ground crew member shows approval of the nose art on 'Touch of Texas'. She was named by her pilot, Captain Bill Denton, in honour of his wife Helen. Denton flew this Liberator on the hazardous low-level strike against the Ploesti oil refineries in Rumania. The horizontal bomb on the mission scoreboard beneath the cockpit represents this mission. The 'doubled-up' nose guns can be seen here.**

Below: **In an attempt to improve exterior visibility for navigators, various styles of scanning windows were devised and field fitted. This version was considered a success by various navigators and the drawings were sent back to the USA where the Ford company started using this type of bulged scanning window on their production line. It first appeared on their B-24Ls and Ms in late 1944. Here is 'Sad Sack' B-24 J-55-CO that flew with the 566th BS as RR=1+ and eventually became the second 389th BG assembly ship. The small projection in front of the window is the lens for the navigator's drift meter.**

Just arrived at Hethel in the Spring of 1944 B-24 J-145-CO (44-40052) EE-O glistens in the sunshine above the scattered clouds. She served with the 565th BS and was one of the first unpainted 'Libs' in the group. To conform with the markings on the olive-drab camouflaged planes, the fuselage codes were painted in grey and the outer tails painted in olive-drab with white disc and yellow serial number and call letter. Very few planes were painted like this as the markings soon gave way to black codes, serials and call letters, with the dark blue disc and white group letter on the natural aluminium skin. This was in turn replaced with all painted vertical tails in late May; in the case of the 389th black with vertical white stripe. She survived combat only to go missing over the continent on 12th May 1945.

Right: 'Ole Buckshot' B-24 J-1-FO (42-50739) of the 567th BS, releases her lethal cargo. *Above*: The port side of the nose of 'Ole Buckshot' which was later transferred to the 491st BG.

Right: The 389th also had a 'tiger faced' Liberator in the shape of B-24 H-25-FO (42-95227) 'Sibonnette' RR-J+. She was badly damaged when she crash landed at the RAF Halifax base at Leconfield, Yorkshire on 3rd February 1945.

Above: **Formerly a 93rd Bomb Group aircraft, 'Jo-Jo's Special Delivery' B-24 D-1-CO (41-23683) became the assembly ship for the 389th Bomb Group. She was stripped down to natural metal and painted with green and yellow stripes.**

Above and right: **The top wing and horizontal tails retained the original olive-drab finish between the yellow and green areas. She was re-named 'The Green Dragon' after a popular pub in nearby Wymondham.**

Below: **After 'The Green Dragon' was salvaged following a crash landing at Manston, Kent on 25th July 1944, the veteran 'The Sad Sack' B-24 J-55-CO (42-99972) replaced her. This plane was painted overall in green and yellow zigzags and had her nose turret replaced by a glazed fairing. Although assembly ships were usually stripped of all armament it can be seen that 'The Green Dragon' retained her top turret and tail guns. On rare occasions these aircraft accompanied their parent groups on combat missions.**

392nd

BOMB GROUP
392nd Bombardment Group (H)

Component Squadrons

Squadron	Code
576th Sqn	C1
577th Sqn	DC
578th Sqn	EC
579th Sqn	GC

Operational base:
Wendling, Norfolk.

First mission
9th September 1943
Last mission
25th April 1945

Total Combat Missions
285 missions

Group Markings
A white disc containing a dark blue, sometimes black, D on the outer vertical tails and upper right wing. From late May 1944 vertical tails were painted white or silver with a black horizontal band.

Above: **A beautiful study of a pristine, almost factory fresh, early Ford built H model 'Poop Deck Pappy' B-24 H-1-FO (42-7521) of the 577th BS. Very soon after her debut with the 392nd BG she was transferred to the 44th BG at Shipdham, then to the 448th at Seething. Points of interest include the very wavy demarcation between olive-drab and neutral grey paintwork - a feature of Ford built aircraft and the large national insignia outlined in red that soon gave way to a dark blue outline. The first batch of H versions from Ford went to the 392nd that introduced the nose-turreted model to the Eighth Air Force.**

Below: **'Pallas Athene - the GI Jane' was christened in honour of the WACs and featured their badge, the Greek Goddess Athene. She was B-24 J-80-CO (42-100187) V and flew with the 578th Squadron and survived the war.**

Below: **Although most of their early 'Libs' were the H version there were a few J models at Wendling. Amongst them was 'Double Trouble' B-24 J-70-CO (42-100100) shown here after ten missions. She had the early Consolidated A-6A nose turret and braced pitot tubes. 'Double Trouble' succumbed to flak over Holland on 29th April 1944.**

25

Left: **Another example of an early Wendling Ford built H, 'Axis Grinder' (B-24 H-1-FO, 42-7495) on her way to the target. The ball turret gunner has his turret traversed forward. She served with the 577th Bomb Squadron and survived the war.**

Below: **Nose art of 'Rose of Jaurez' and 'Short Snorter'. The Pegasus emblem on 'Short Snorter' is in red.**

Below: **High over the coast a San Diego built J and a Willow Run built H. The nearest plane is 'Rose of Jaurez' (B-24 H-1-FO, 42-7469) of the 579th Bomb Squadron. The other plane is 'Short Snorter' (B-24 J-60-CO, 42-99990) which completed over 100 missions.**

Right: Most combat groups had a 'Ford's Folly' in their ranks and the 392nd was no exception. She was B-24 H-1-FO (42-7466) EC-W of the 578th Bomb Squadron, seen here early in her career with nine missions marked up.

Right: Several weeks later 'Ford's Folly' had completed thirty-six missions. She has also acquired armour plate beneath the cockpit. The last three digits of her serial are in yellow on her nose and a scanning blister window had been added. The ordnance crew are handling fragmentation clusters, a most unpopular cargo. 'Ford's Folly' ended her days over Koblenz on the Hannover mission of 11th September 1944 when she was shot down by fighters.

Below: For the hard working ground crews out on the dispersal areas, the arrival of the YMCA coffee wagon was always a welcome event, especially on a cold winter's day. At Wendling it was appreciated so much that they named a Liberator in honour of the good ladies who manned the van. 'The YMCA Flying Service' was B-24 H-10-DT (41-28700) and flew with both the 577th Bomb Squadron and 579th Bomb Squadron before transferring to the 492nd Bomb Group (second organisation).

Above: **250 pounders cascade from 'We'll Get By' B-24 J-1-FO (42-50697). The three bulges below the nose section are the covers for the radar countermeasure antennas which were fitted to many B-24s during the latter part of 1944.**

Left: **The nose art of 'We'll Get By' that survived the war.**

Below: **'American Beauty' from the 578th Squadron completes her landing run at Wendling during the summer of 1944. Note the flarepath lights in the foreground and the P-47 group formation monitor in the background. B-24 H-30-FO (42-95293) was lost over Misburg on 4th November 1944.**

Above: 'Ruptured Duck' B-24 H-15-FO (42-52770) displays a distinctively well-worn look towards the end of her long career. Note the replacement engine cowlings, field-fitted three piece waist windows and de-icer boots removed. Here the nose art has been over-painted, but the inset shows how it used to be although the extra armour has docked its tail!

Above: The 392nd Bomb Group acquired B-24 D-1-CO (41-23689) 'Minerva' from the 44th Bomb Group and painted it white on the top surfaces with white images of B-24 noses on the front fuselage and an image of a tail turret aft of the national insignia.

445th
BOMB GROUP
445th Bombardment Group (H)

Component Squadrons

Squadron	Code
700th Sqn	1S
701st Sqn	MK
702nd Sqn	WV
703rd Sqn	RN

Operational base:
Wendling, Norfolk.

First mission
13th December 1943
Last mission
25th April 1945

Total Combat Missions
282 missions

Group Markings
A white disc containing a dark blue, sometimes black, F on the outer vertical tails and upper right wing. From late May 1944 vertical tails were painted white or black with a white horizontal band.

Above: **'Conquest Cavalier' was one of the 445th Bomb Group's original planes and flew with the 701st Squadron. She was photographed in the Spring of 1944.**

Below: **'Conquest Cavalier' (B-24 H-1-CF, 42-29126) again. A number 9 can be seen on the inside of the outer-left engine cowling and 3 was carried on the opposite engine; These were reference points for the top turret gunner when crew members were calling out attacking enemy fighters and using the 'clock' system of sighting. This aircraft was eventually transferred to the 446th Bomb Group.**

Above: 'Skipper's Clipper' a Ford built B-24 H-20-FO (42-95000) heavily loaded with flexing wings; disconcerting to inexperienced crew members.

Below: 'The Grim Reaper' from the 701st Bomb Squadron. The 445th Group repeated their Liberator's call letters on the fuselage sides aft of the squadron codes, usually in yellow. 'The Grim Reaper' was San Diego built B-24 J-100-CO and survived the war.

31

Left: In plan-form the Liberator could look graceful, as here where the slender 110 foot span of the Davis wing is seen to advantage. This is an H model from the 445th Bomb Group.

Left: Resting between missions at Tibenham, B-24 J-1-FO (42-50732) from the 700th Bomb Squadron. This plane also survived hostilities.

Below: 'Lonesome Lois' B24 H-20-FO, crash landed at RAF Beccles, Suffolk, on 13th July 1944 and over-ran the runway where her nose wheel collapsed on the rough ground. Note the fully enclosed waist windows that were introduced at 'block 20' on the production line. The waist gun is now fitted in a swivel mount directly below the window, this arrangement was far more comfortable for the gunners.
Inset: 'Lonesome Lois' had repairs made to the underside of the nose.

'GATOR' B-24 H-1-FO (42-7516) 458th Bomb Group

On 20th September 1944 whilst engaged in a 'gasoline trucking' mission to Lille, Gator failed to gain altitude after taking off from Horsham St Faith. She stalled and crashed in Hastings Avenue, Hellesdon, Norwich.

'THE HELL WAGON' B-24 H-1-FO (42-7492) 392nd Bomb Group

One of the 392nd's original 'H' versions, she was later assigned to the 453rd Bomb Group.

'TOMMY THUMPER II' B-24 H-20-FO (42-94811) 34th Bomb Group

After the 34th BG converted to the B-17, Tommy Thumper II went to the 467th BG. She crashed during a training flight at Old Catton, Norwich on 22nd January 1945.

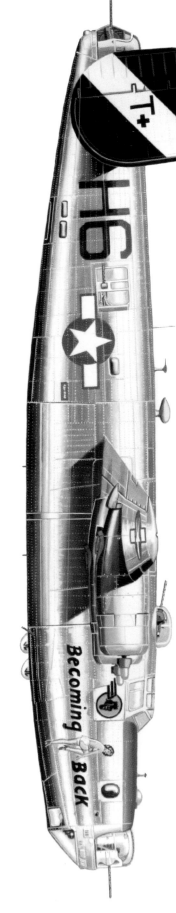

BECOMING BACK B-24 J-85-CF (44-10375) 453rd Bomb Group

After flying most of her missions with the 453rd BG, she was transferred to the 491st BG in April 1945 and lived up to her name by returning to the USA at the end of the war.

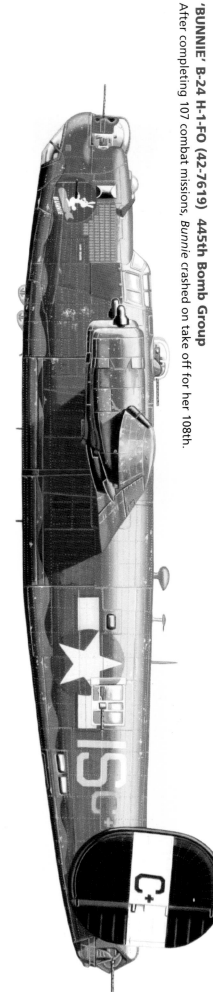

'BUNNIE' B-24 H-1-FO (42-7619) 445th Bomb Group

After completing 107 combat missions, *Bunnie* crashed on take off for her 108th.

'PARSON'S CHARIOT' B-24 J-140-CO (42-110162) 466th Bomb Group

Originally assigned to the 491st BG, she commenced operations with the 466th BG on 6th June 1944. After landing from a mission to Brunswick on 31st March 1945, she caught fire and was destroyed.

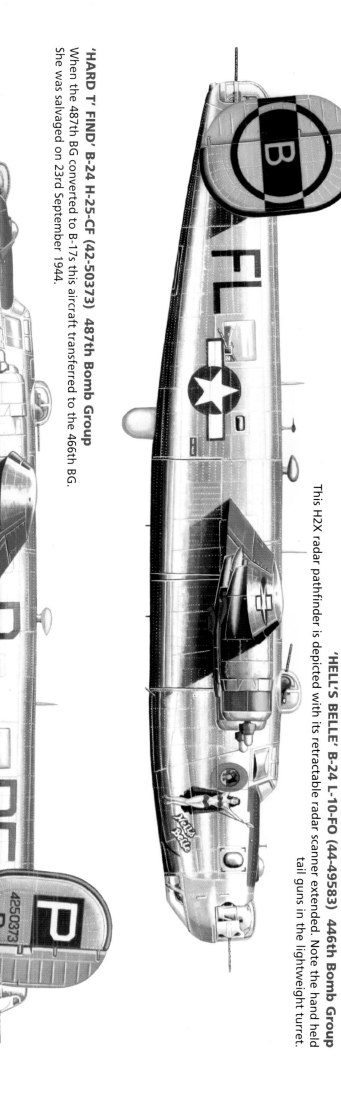

'HELL'S BELLE' B-24 L-10-FO (44-49583) 446th Bomb Group

This H2X radar pathfinder is depicted with its retractable radar scanner extended. Note the hand held tail guns in the lightweight turret.

'HARD T' FIND' B-24 H-25-CF (42-50373) 487th Bomb Group

When the 487th BG converted to B-17s this aircraft transferred to the 466th BG. She was salvaged on 23rd September 1944.

'OLD IRONPANTS' (THE PERFECT LADY) B-24 J-140-CO (42-110168) 467th Bomb Group

Originally a 491st BG aircraft, she started flying with the 467th BG in early June 1944 and survived the war. She was named in honour of a popular Norwich barmaid well known for her impeccable character!

'SLO' FREIGHT' B-24 J-145-CO (44-40111) 491st Bomb Group
One of the Group's original aircraft, she was damaged on a low-level supply drop to airborne troops in Holland on 18th September 1944.
She made an emergency landing at Woodbridge, Suffolk but suffered a nosewheel collapse on touchdown and was destroyed by fire.

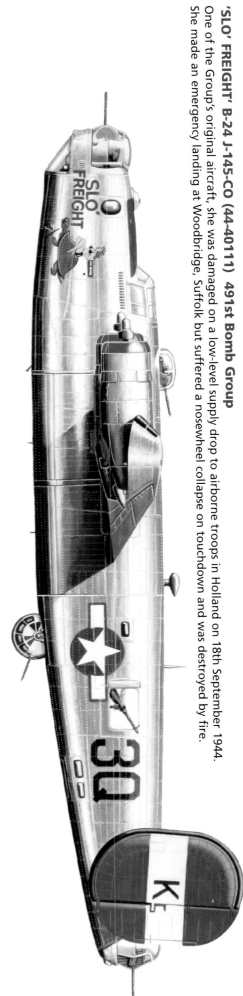

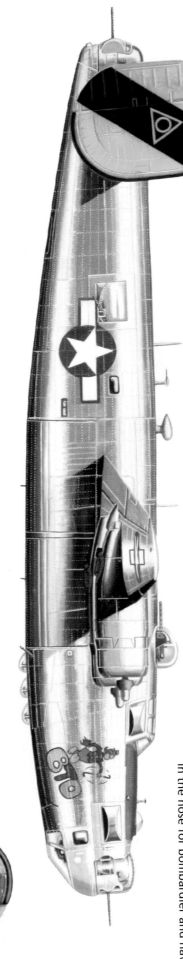

'B.T.O.' (BIG TIME OPERATOR) B-24 M (44-50678) 448th Bomb Group
The final B-24 model to operate with the 8th Air Force. Note the additional windows
in the nose for bombardier and navigator.

'SWEATER GAL' B-24 J-75-CO (42-100150) 93rd Bomb Group
This veteran flew no less than 75 missions with the 93rd BG and is fitted with the early Consolidated nose turret.
She was salvaged as 'war weary' at the end of hostilities.

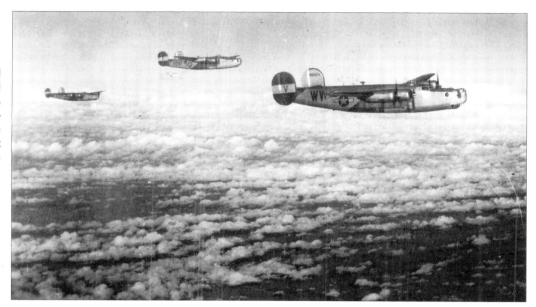

Right: **Three 445th Libs head for the target over scattered cloud. The nearest plane is 'Stormy' B-24 J-1-FO (42-50574) of the 702nd Bomb Squadron, whilst on her left is 'Hitler's Hearse' of the 703rd Squadron.**

Above: **Two views of the 'Silver Streak', a B-24 H-25-FO (42-95192) of the 703rd Bomb Squadron after a nose wheel failure on 28th May 1944. She was repaired, but failed to return from her 31st mission; to Periers, France, on 25th July 1944. Note the light coloured squadron codes, which could have been yellow as the 445th chose to use the colour on a number of their planes for some reason.**

Right: **Formerly 'Lucky Gordon' of the 93rd Bomb Group B-24 D-20-CO (41-24215) became the 'Judas Goat' for the 445th Bomb Group at Tibenham. She was finished in broad black and orange stripes and a reclining female graced the right nose of this plane. The officer (inset) is Captain W Strawinski of the 701st Bomb Squadron, 445th Bomb Group.**

446th

BOMB GROUP

446th Bombardment Group (H)

Component Squadrons
Squadron	Code
704th Sqn	FL
705th Sqn	HN
706nd Sqn	RT
707th Sqn	JU

Operational base:
Bungay, Suffolk.

First mission
16th December 1943
Last mission
25th April 1945

Total Combat Missions
273 missions

Group Markings
A white disc containing a dark blue, sometimes black, H on the outer vertical tails and upper right wing. From late May 1944 vertical tails were painted deep yellow with a black horizontal band. From June 1944 coloured engine cowl bands were in evidence:

Red	704th Sqn
Yellow	705th Sqn
White	706th Sqn
Blue	707th Sqn

From late Summer 1944 Pathfinder B-24s were distinguished by a yellow and black circle superimposed over the existing coloured tails.

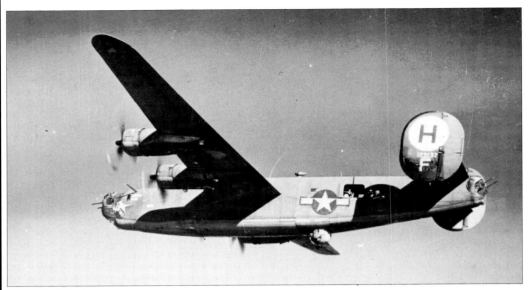

Above: 'Dry Run' B-24 H-1-CF (41-29137) of the 706th Bomb Squadron. San Diego and Fort Worth built B-24s had different styles of paint finish. The demarcation between the olive-drab and grey was in a regular line compared to the wavy line of the Ford models. 'Dry Run' was lost over Bussin, Germany, on 4th August 1944.

Above: 'Star Dust' of the 705th Bomb Squadron B-24 H-1-FO (42-7576) another lucky Lib that survived the war.

Above: The nose of 'Star Dust' after 27 missions. The navigator's blister window, seen here, was actually a discarded cockpit side blister. Quite a few aircraft had these relocated over the small navigator's window allowing an improved field of vision. This feature was only seen on the 446th Bomb Group's planes.

Right: **A formation of the 446th sets out over the North Sea early in 1944. Nearest plane is 'Old Faithful' with 'Lazy Lou' above and 'The Spirit of 77' immediately below.**

Below: **Nose detail of the same three Libs:**
'Old Faithful' B-24 H-1-FO (42-7505) of the 706th Bomb Squadron crashed at Bungay on 28th August 1944.
'Lazy Lou' B-24 H-1-FO (42-7609) of the 706th Bomb Squadron was transferred to the 36th Bomb Squadron (RCM).
'The Spirit of 77' B-24 H-1-FO (42-7607) of the 705th Bomb Squadron also transferred to the 36th Bomb Squadron (RCM).

Right: **The famous 'Red Ass' B-24 H-25-FO (42-95203) FL-D of the 704th Bomb Squadron. Various sources claim this plane was the first Eighth Air Force bomber over the D-Day beaches on 6th June 1944. She survived the war.**

Above: A very famous Liberator was 'Ronnie' B-24 H-1-CF (41-29144). This 704th Bomb Squadron machine was named in honour of S/Sgt Ronald Gannon of the 446th who was taken ill and died whilst the group were in training in the USA. The plane went on to complete no less than 119 combat missions.

Left: A battle scarred veteran of the 706th Bomb Squadron was 'Homebreaker' B-24 H-15-FO (42-52612) that carried on to survive the war. She was photographed at altitude on her 100th combat mission, on 10th April 1945. The elements, especially ice, could be hard on the paintwork and hail stones could reduce portions of the airframe to bare metal very rapidly.

Above: **'Going My Way?' B-24 J-60-CF (44-10528) on the Magdeburg mission of 6th February 1945, with Lieutenant Carl Gjelhaug at the controls. Carl flew this Liberator back across the Atlantic at the war's end.**

Left: **Lieutenant Carl Gjelhaug (in fur collared jacket) and some of his crew pose before 'Going My Way?' their usual mount. Carl was one of the youngest airplane commanders at Bungay. He went on to make a career in the US Air Force and later flew B-29s in Korea, B47s and much later, B-52s over Vietnam.**

Right: **In contrast to the battered veterans, the brand new, gleaming, 'Mighty Mouse' roars his defiance. One of the last models from Ford B-24 M-10-FO (44-50775) FL-M of the 704th Bomb Squadron incorporated large navigator's scanning windows.**

Above: 'Eager Beaver' B-24 D-1-CO (41-23737 formerly of the 93rd Bomb Group, was selected as the assembly ship for the 446th Bomb Group. She was painted overall in international orange, a colour selected by Lieutenant Colonel Frederick Knorre, the group operations officer, and named 'Fearless Freddie' in his honour.

Left: The nose art of 'Fearless Freddie'. The lad sitting on the black bomb is superimposed against a blue disc, the word 'fearless' is in blue whilst 'Freddie' is in black.

Left: Later in the war 'Fearless Freddie' had a yellow tail with black horizontal band.

448th Bombardment Group (H)

Component Squadrons

Squadron	Code
712th Sqn	CT
713th Sqn	IG
714nd Sqn	EI
715th Sqn	IO

Operational base:
Seething, Norfolk.

First mission
22nd December 1943
Last mission
25th April 1945

Total Combat Missions
262 missions

Group Markings
A white disc containing a dark blue, sometimes black, I on the outer vertical tails and upper right wing. From late May 1944 vertical tails were painted deep yellow with a black diagonal band.

On this group, squadrons were further identified by a squadron symbol surrounding the individual call-letter.

712th Sqn -Triangle
713rd Sqn - Circle
714th Sqn - Square
715th Sqn - Diamond

Above: **The 448th sets out on one of its early missions. This photo illustrates well the unique squadron symbols used on the tails in this group. The nearest plane is 'Lady from Bristol' B-24 H-5-FO (42-52100) of the 714th Squadron. She carried the call letter F within a square, symbol for the 714th. She was lost on 25th February 1944 on a mission to Amiens, France.**

Above: **'The Flying Sac' B-24 J-135-CO (42-110098) sporting the diamond tail symbol of the 715th Squadron. She was photographed at Dubendorf, Switzerland, where she landed after being damaged in combat on 24th April 1944.**

Left: **The characters from Al Capp's comic strip 'Dogpatch' were popular with Eighth Air Force crews. 'Daisy Mae!!' was one of the prettier ones; officially B-24 F-20-FO (42-94972) CT-M of the 712th Squadron.**

Left: **Nine 500 pounders cascade from the bomb bay of 'Brownie', a B-24 J-5-FO (42-50809) of the 714th Squadron. Note the blisters for the RCM aerials beneath the nose. In the J-5 block the glazed waist windows were deepened and the gun mount incorporated in the actual glazing.**

Left: **'Sonia' a B-24 H-25-FO sustained flak damage on the 19th October 1944 mission to Gustavsburg, Germany, but was repaired and saw out the rest of the war.**

Below: **'Fat Stuff II' B-24 H-1-FO (42-7591) trundles along the Seething perimeter track. When taxiing a B-24 it was normal practice for a crew member, usually the flight engineer, to sit or stand in the top hatch to advise pilots of obstacles which could be snagged by the wingtips. She was attached to the 712th Squadron and ended her war in Switzerland when she limped to Altenrhein severely damaged after combat on 12th July 1944.**

Right: **The 448th also had a Lib with the tiger's head, this time adorning the nose of 'Rugged But Right' B-24 H-20-FO (42-94953) of the 715th Squadron. She had previously served with the 492nd Bomb Group and flew back to the USA at the end of the war.**

Below: **One of the first unpainted, natural silver Libs at Seething was 'Tarfu' B-24 J-145-CO (44-40099) of the 712th Squadron. She was photographed when visiting Wendling in her interim tail markings. She was lost over Germany on 25th March 1945.**

Above: 'Mickey Ship' B-24 J-1-FO (42-50587) of the 712th Squadron, with her H2X radome lowered, heads for the target. She force landed on the continent on 11th December 1944 on the Hanau mission and was salvaged.

Above: 'Achtung! Noon Balloon' B-24 M-5-FO (44-50540) EI-K of the 714th Squadron was another B-24 that survived the war.

Left: Two views of B-24 J-1-FO (42-95527) '4F'. 4F was the medical category which declared a man unfit for military service! Unfit or not, she survived the war with the 712nd Bomb Squadron.

Above: Painted in yellow and black chequers 'You Cawn't miss it' displays her plumage. Another ex- 93rd Bomb Group B-24 D-5-CO (41-23809) 'Hellsadroppin II' she was used as the 448th Bomb Group assembly ship. Assembly duty was not the only function these planes performed as they were used as hacks for transportation and other jobs.

Below and right: The replacement for 'You Cawn't miss it', B-24 H-15-CF (41-29489) originally named '2nd Avenue El' she was painted in maroon and white segments divided by black lines.

453rd
BOMB GROUP
453rd Bombardment Group (H)

Component Squadrons

Squadron	Code
732nd Sqn	E3
733rd Sqn	F8
734th Sqn	E8
735th Sqn	H6

Operational base:
Old Buckenham, Norfolk.

First mission
5th February 1944
Last mission
12th April 1945

Total Combat Missions
259 missions

Group Markings
A white disc containing a dark blue, sometimes black, J on the outer vertical tails and upper right wing. From late May 1944 vertical tails were painted black with a white diagonal band.

On this group, squadrons were further identified by coloured propeller spinners:

White	732nd Sqn
Blue	733rd Sqn
Red	734th Sqn
Yellow	735th Sqn

Many Liberators in this group did not carry squadron code letters on the fuselage.

Above: 'The Golden Gaboon' B-24 H-5-DT (41-28645) a Douglas-Tulsa built H model. On 30th May 1944 she crash-landed and caught fire arriving home from the Oldenburg mission. Douglas built Hs had a wavy demarcation between the olive-drab and grey, but not nearly as pronounced as their Ford built contempories.

Right: A much weathered 'Cabin in the Sky' B-24 H-10-CF on a practice mission (note the lack of waist guns). She had recently acquired a replacement left rudder which had yet to be painted with the rear segment of the white disc. She served with the 735th Squadron and was lost on 27th March 1944.

Right: 'Libby Raider' B-24 H-5-DT (41-28642) E8-I+ of the 734th Squadron was a Tulsa built model and crash landed at Old Buckenham on 2nd March 1944.

44

Above: **Three H models from the 732nd Bomb Squadron holding a tight formation. Leading the element is 'Battle Package' (42-52201) which was lost on the 11th July 1944 Munich mission. Nearest is 'El Flako' lost on its 78th mission. On the far side is 'Ken O Kay II' B-24 H-10-FO (42-52301) lost on 29th April 1944 when she ditched in the sea 30 miles east of Great Yarmouth after sustaining damage from Flak and fighters.**

Below and right: **Two more views of 'El Flako' B-24 H-10-CF (42-64469) taken in the summer of 1944, showing signs of wear and tear. She went on to complete 77 missions, but received a direct Flak hit on the 78th mission, 2nd November 1944, and broke in half in the air.**

Above and right: 'Foil Proof' B-24 H-20-FO (42-94805) another veteran which flew no less than 108 missions from Old Buckenham.

Below: Three Liberators from the 733rd Bomb Squadron en-route to their target. Nearest is 'Whiskey Jingles' B-24 H-25-DT (42-51114). Note how the wing tips flex upwards, a characteristic of a heavily loaded Liberator.

Inset: The nose of 'Whiskey Jingles'. The line at left is the red propeller warning indicator, a marking seldom seen on B-24s. She also survived the war.

Right: 'Linda Lou' B-24 J-5-FO (42-50764) of the 735th Bomb Squadron undergoing an engine change during the severe winter of 1944-45. She later transferred to the 448th Bomb Group.

Right: Students of the Liberator could be bemused by this photo, but 'Mary Harriet' was in fact a San Diego Built B-24 J-140-CO (42-110149) formerly of the 491st Bomb Group. She had her original Motor Products nose turret replaced with an Emerson version.

Below: 112 mission symbols on the nose of 'Spirit of Notre Dame' B-24 H-25-FO (42-95102) of the 734th Bomb Squadron. When the 453rd Bomb Group ceased operations on 12th April 1945 she went to Seething to join the 448th.

Left: 'Wham Bam' B-24 D-1-CO (41-23738) originally went to war with the 93rd Bomb Group. When the 453rd at Old Buckenham took her on as their 'Judas Goat' they alternated large yellow squares with squares of her original finish and retained her nose art.

Right: **A mechanic tends one of Wham Bam's engines, affording a close-up of the nose art.**

Left: Worn and tired late in her career she has replacement engine cowlings, new tail markings and a new left bomb door.

Component Squadrons

Squadron	Code
752nd Sqn	7V
753rd Sqn	J4
754th Sqn	Z5
755th Sqn	J3

Operational base:
Horsham St Faith,
Norfolk.

First mission
24th February 1944
Last mission
25th April 1945

Total Combat Missions
240 missions

Group Markings
A white disc containing a dark
blue, sometimes black, K on
the outer vertical tails and
upper right wing. From late
May 1944 vertical tails were
painted red with a white vertical band.

Above: **During the summer of 1944 the 753rd Bomb Squadron was selected to test a new guided weapon, the Azon bomb. Ten new B-24Js arrived from the USA modified to operate this device whilst existing squadron aircraft were fitted out in the field. One of these was 'Times-a-Wastin' B-24 J-140-CO (42-110163). The three Azon aerials can be seen below the rear fuselage. The Azon experiment was reasonably successful, but weather conditions over Europe were rarely suitable for this type of operation to be a viable proposition. The B-24s of the 753rd Bomb Squadron were converted back for conventional bombing operations. 'Times-a-Wastin' carries the cartoon character 'Snuffy Smith' on her nose.**

Left: **Twins Don and John Echols served at Horsham St Faith in the same squadron and sometimes even in the same aircraft. Both survived, although Don was wounded by Flak. Here they are posing with 'Rough Riders'.**

Right: **Taken from the waist window of the 458th's first assembly ship 'First Sergeant' B-24 J-95-CO (42-100365) passes over the Norfolk coast at Overstrand. She was attached to the 752nd Bomb Squadron and was lost on the 12th July 1944 Munich mission.**

Above: **An excellent view of Horsham St Faith with 'Shack Time' B-24 J-155-CO (44-40275) heading northwards over the base. Members of the 458th were in many ways luckier than most Eighth Air Force personnel as they were housed in comfortable, heated quarters and the historic city of Norwich, noted for its many public houses and dance halls as well as its rich history, was just a short cycle ride away. 'Shack Time' was salvaged at the base on 12th November 1944.**

Left and below: **Captain Curt Vogel and crew brought over 'Rough Riders' B-24 H-15-CF (41-29342) with the group. She was unusual in having artwork on her rear fuselage as well as her nose section. She flew with the 755th Bomb Squadron as J3-S.**

Left: **The Curt Vogel crew pose before 'Princess Pat' B-24 H-30-FO (42-95316) J3-N.**
They were, left to right: Back row, 1st Lt Samuel D Scorza (navigator), 1st Lt Curt M Vogel (pilot), 1st Lt Allen C Hillborn (co-pilot), 1st Lt Alex J Testa (bombardier). Front row, S/Sgt Albert W. Walczak (waist gunner), T/Sgt Bernard J Doyle (radio operator), T/Sgt Joseph R Brown (top turret gunner/engineer) S/Sgt Raymond J Potts (ball turret gunner), S/Sgt Lovell T West (waist gunner).

Right: 'Silver Chief' B-24 J-150-CO (44-40201), a former Azon machine, now with aerials removed. She started her combat career with the 492nd Bomb Group and eventually force-landed on the continent on 10th January 1945.

Below right: 'Silver Chief' had an unusual field modification, an added sheet of metal in place of Plexiglass on the side of her MTP A-6-B nose turret.

Above: 'Lily Marlene' B-24 J-5-FO (42-50907) 'D' from the 755th Bomb Squadron. The famous Norden bomb sight used in J model lead ships such as 'Lily' was top secret and whilst on the ground it had to be shrouded with a special cover. However, somebody has slipped up here as the sight is in full view. Some people might consider the young lady is also in need of a little touch of modesty. She was lost when she crashed and exploded at Crowland, Peterborough, on 9th September 1944.

Right: That well known nose again, this time of B-24 J-100-CO (42-100408) J4-I of the 753rd Bomb Squadron. She survived the hostilities.

Left: Tight formation keeping by two 458th Bomb Group 'Libs'. The nearest is 'Dorothy Kay Special' from the 754th Bomb Squadron, B-24 J-401-CF (42-50456) that completed 70 missions by VE-Day. Off her right wing flies B-24 J-1-FO (42-95610) of the 752nd Bomb Squadron.

Left: 'The Shack' B-24 J-160-CO (44-40298) of the 754th Bomb Squadron, commences her take off run late in 1944. The usual black rubber de-icer boots on the leading edge of the wings and tailplane are lacking because Consolidated at San Diego switched over to thermal de-icing at 'J block 150'. The open waist-gun hatches have been fitted with three-piece waist windows, a field modification of the winter of 1944-45. The windows were produced in kit form by the St Paul modification centre.

Left: 'Final Approach' B-24 H-15-FO (42-52457) 7V-Q of the 752nd Bomb Squadron had flown 122 missions by 9th April 1945 when she was downed on her 123rd. A newly fitted navigator's blister window obscures the first letter of her name.

Above: The first assembly ship to serve with the 458th Bomb Group was B-24 D-30-CO (42-40127) from the 93rd Bomb Group 'Thar She Blows Again'. She was given a very elaborate paint job at Horsham St Faith and re-named 'First Sergeant' although this did not appear on the plane. She was painted white on her forward fuselage and upper wing surfaces, but left natural drab on her rear fuselage. Later the white areas were covered in dark blue and red spots while red and yellow spots adorned the olive drab section.

Right and below: **A fire destroyed 'First Sergeant' in late May 1944 and she burnt out on the airfield. She was replaced by the similarly decorated B-24 H-20-DT (41-28967) from the 754th Squadron. In March 1945 she was involved in a crash landing that ended her career. She was usually known as 'The Spotted Ape' and both were at times referred to as 'Wonder Bird' after Wonder Bread, an American bread that came in white wrappers with red and blue spots.**

466th
BOMB GROUP
466th Bombardment Group (H)

Component Squadrons

Squadron	Code
784th Sqn	T9
785th Sqn	2U
786th Sqn	U8
787th Sqn	6L

Operational base:
Attlebridge, Norfolk.

First mission
22nd March 1944
Last mission
25th April 1945

Total Combat Missions
232 missions

Group Markings
A white disc containing a dark blue, sometimes black, L on the outer vertical tails and upper right wing. From late May 1944 vertical tails were painted red with a white horizontal band.

Above: 'Jamaica' B-24 H-10-DT (41-28746) of the 785th Bomb Squadron lifts off from Attlebridge in her early tail markings.

Right: 'Jamaica' sported elaborate and well executed nose art on both sides of her nose.

Below: On a mission to Evreux, France, on 15th June 1944 she was damaged by Flak but managed to put down on a fighter strip in Normandy. She was eventually lost on 25th September 1944 whilst on a gasoline tanking operation to France.

54

Right: **Resting in the sun at Attlebridge 'Laden Maid' B-24 H-15-FO (42-52560) of the 786th Bomb Squadron. She was salvaged on the last day of 1944.
Inset: Close-up of her artwork early in her career after five combat missions.**

Below: **Along with many other Second Bomb Division B-24s, 'Miss Minooky' B-24 H-30-CF (42-50438) delivers gasoline for General Patton's army in Europe. In September 1944 many Liberators were employed on this vital task. 'Miss Minooky' flew with the 786th Bomb Squadron and carried the yellow cowl rings to the end of the war.**

Above: **Three views of 'The Falcon' B-24 H-25-FO (42-95248) 2U-S from the 785th Bomb Squadron. She carried a very unusual nose decoration in black paint and blue engine cowls, which were normal squadron markings. 'The Falcon' crash landed at Shipdham on 8th January 1945 and finished up with her nose section partly submerged in an ice covered pond.**

Left: **With Fowler flaps lowered 'Snafu Snark' slows down during her landing run at Attlebridge early in her career.**
Inset: Fearsom shark's teeth on 'The Snafu Snark' B-24 H-15-CF (41-29387) 2U-B+.

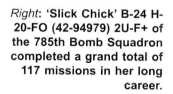

Above: **With her H2X scanner lowered 'Fran' B-24 L-10-FO (44-49582) of the 785th Bomb Squadron leads the formation on the target approach late in the war. H2X was an American refinement of the RAF's H2S.**

Inset: **'Fran' was painted in red with a black shadow. The projection beneath the bubble window was the navigator's drift meter lens which was moved to the left side on the 'L' model.**

Right: **'Slick Chick' B-24 H-20-FO (42-94979) 2U-F+ of the 785th Bomb Squadron completed a grand total of 117 missions in her long career.**

Left: **The 466th Bomb Group Attlebridge assembly ship was decorated in a spectacular manner. Originally know as 'Ready and Willing' B-24 D-20-CO (41-24109) had flown with the 44th and 93rd Bomb Groups. When the 466th took her over she was stripped down to natural metal and painted in red zigzags overall.**

Above: **Later she acquired the red and white tail markings plus an array of signal lights over her national insignia in the form of a large L – the group letter.**

Left: **In May 1945 she came under the 787th Bomb Squadron instead of the 784th hence the change of codes from T9 to 6L. She has also been re-fitted with de-icer boots on her tailplane and been given glazed three piece waist windows.**

467th
BOMB GROUP
467th Bombardment Group (H)

Component Squadrons

Squadron	Code
788th Sqn	X7
789th Sqn	6A
790th Sqn	Q2
791st Sqn	4Z

Operational base:
Rackheath, Norfolk.

First mission
10th April 1944
Last mission
25th April 1945

Total Combat Missions
212 missions

Group Markings
A white disc containing a dark blue, sometimes black, P on the outer vertical tails and upper right wing. From late May 1944 vertical tails were painted red with a white diagonal band.
Late in 1944 many of the group's 'Libs' had the last three digits of their serial number painted in large numbers on the nose.

Above: 'Double Trouble' B-24 H-15-CF (41-29385) flew as 4Z-H+ with the 791st Bomb Squadron and Q2-S with the 790th. She survived the war, but was salvaged as war-weary after hostilities.

Below: Two views of 'Tailwind' B-24 H-15-CF (41-29369) of the 789th Bomb Squadron that went down in the North Sea returning from the 11th July 1944 Munich mission. The overly blotchy appearance of her olive-drab is due to repainting after severe icing conditions removed much of her paint.

Above: **An almost new B-24 H-25-FO (42-95273) Q2-I of the 790th Bomb Squadron on its fourth combat mission lets loose 6,000 pounds of explosive ordnance in the spring of 1944. Within a split second her companions will release their cargoes. The planes in the background include 'Snooper' B-24 H-15-FO (42-52571) Q2-D in front and 'Witch-craft' top right.**

Below: **A peaceful scene at Rackheath as 'Wolves Inc' B-24 H-20-DT (41-28981) rests on its hardstand with the Salhouse Road railway crossing in the right background. 'Wolves Inc' had to ditch 10 miles off Cromer on return from the 4th March 1945 Stuttgart mission.**

Above and right: **The Eighth Air Force's champion Liberator, the famous 'Witchcraft' B-24 H-15-FO (42-52534) of the 790th Bomb Squadron after completing 100 missions with (right) her eventual record tally of 130.**

Above: **Up for a practice mission on a bright summer's day, two B-24s from the 790th Bomb Squadron formate over a pastoral landscape with Gorleston to the top left of the picture. Nearest is 'Tangerine' B-24 H-15-CF (41-29446) with 'Valiant Lady' H-15-CF (41-29408). 'Tangerine', from the title of a popular song of the time, was salvaged on the continent on 14th November 1944.**

Below: **Flaring-out and a split second from touch-down with another 'Lib' on the crosswind leg, B-24 L-10-FO (44-49591) 4Z-H+ arrives back on the Rackheath runway. She was a PFF lead ship, as were many B-24Ls. Eighth Air Force Ls carried the lightweight hand-held tail gun position which saved weight and allowed for the fitting of the H2X Radar amidships.**

Above: **Several Liberators in the 467th Bomb Group had the last three digits of the serial number repeated on the nose, this is a good example. 'Liberty Run' B-24 M-10-FO (44-50668) from the 791st Bomb Squadron had an extra bubble window for the bombardier as well as a large scanning window for the navigator.**

Above: At Rackheath the 467th Bomb Group had two assembly ships which were almost identical. Both were black overall with large yellow discs outlined in red and carrying the name 'Pete the P.O.M. Inspector' and 'Pete the P.O.M. Inspector 2nd'. The first was ex 44th and 389th Bomb Group B-24 D-55-CO (42-40370) formerly 'Heaven Can Wait'. After a landing mishap at Rackheath it was replaced by B-24 H-15-CF (41-29393) previously known as 'Shoo Shoo Baby'.

Below: The replacement for 'Pete the P.O.M. Inspector' was B-24 H-15-CF (41-29393) 'Pete the P.O.M. Inspector 2nd' previously known as 'Shoo Shoo Baby' that had its nose replaced with old type D greenhouse.

489th

BOMB GROUP
489th Bombardment Group (H)

Component Squadrons

Squadron	Code
844th Sqn	4R
845th Sqn	T4
846th Sqn	8R
847th Sqn	S4

Operational base:
Halesworth, Suffolk.

First mission
30th May 1944
Last mission
10th November 1944

Total Combat Missions
106 missions

Group Markings
A white disc containing a dark blue, sometimes black, W on the upper right wing. Vertical tails were painted green with a white vertical band.
In August 1944 the group was transferred from the 95th Combat Wing to the 20th Wing and the outer tails were re-painted deep yellow.

Above: 'The Sharon D' and 'Phoney Express' during formation assembly and displaying their green and white vertical tails. These were changed to all yellow when the group transferred from the 95th Combat Wing to the 20th in August 1944.

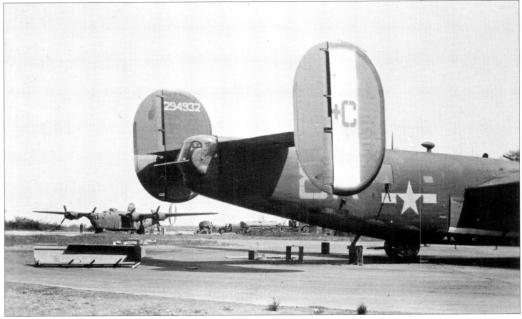

Right: The rear of 'Paper Doll' in the sun at Halesworth, with 'Stubby Gal' in the background. 'Paper Doll' a B-24 H-20-FO of the 846th Bomb Squadron was returning from Kassel on 27th September 1944 when she was in collision with 42-94888 and crashed at Walberswick, Suffolk.

Right: Waiting on the ramp in the USA prior to flying with the 489th Bomb Group to England, one of the originals; B-24 H-20-FO (42-94945). She is in pristine condition and has not yet had any combat modifications carried out. 'Cover Girl' flew with the 846th Bomb Squadron as 8R+B and was lost on the 6th August 1944 Hamburg mission.

Above: As the target is reached and identified the smoke markers and bombs go down from the PFF lead ships. These two Liberators are from the 547th Bomb Squadron and have white H2X radomes below.

Contrasting tail colours. *Left*: 'War Bride' B-24 H-20-FO (42-94924) of the 847th Bomb Squadron that crashed at Halesworth on return from the 25th June 1944 Villacoublay mission displays her green with white tail feathers. *Right*: 'Rum Dum' B-24 H-20-CF (42-50280) of the 845th Bomb Squadron was eventually transferred to the 446th Bomb Group. She sports a new all yellow tail.

Right: 'Rebel Gal' B-24 H-20-FO coasts along the perimeter track with a visiting third division ship in the background. She flew with the 845th Bomb Squadron as T4-S and eventually transferred to the 392nd Bomb Group at Wendling. The light stripes on the lower edge of the bomb doors were a visual indicator to allow other crews in the formation to judge if the doors were open or closed. These stripes were normally white, sometimes yellow on olive-drab and grey planes, and usually yellow on silver ships.

Left: A nice photo of a 845th Squadron Ford built B-24 J-1-FO T4-R about to flare out for landing at Halesworth.

Left: 'The Sharon D' B-24 H-10-FO (42-94759) of the 847th Bomb Squadron eventually transferred to the 445th Bomb Group.

Left: Lieutenant Colonel Leon Vance jr. before leaving with the group for the British Isles had a B-24 christened in honour of his small daughter, Sharon D Vance. Colonel Vance and little Sharon are seen here at the naming ceremony. For his extreme heroism on a mission on 5th June 1944, during which he lost a foot, Vance was awarded the Medal of Honor. After hospitalisation and surgery in England he was being flown back to the USA when the C-54 Skymaster he was a passenger in disappeared over the Atlantic. The Medal of Honor was presented posthumously and handed to Sharon by General Hodges in the USA.

Smoke markers go down as 'Bomber's Moon' (42-94903) reaches her target; Speyerdorf Airfield, Germany, on 3rd October 1944. 'Bomber's Moon', like a large proportion of 489th Bomb Group's original aircraft was a B-24 H-20-FO of the 844th Bomb Squadron. Sixteen days later, on 19th October, she crashed near the target after colliding with 42-94913.

Below:
'Special Delivery' and 'Joe' over scattered cloud and heading for Munster on 25th October 1944. 'Joe' in the rear, was B-24 H-15-FO (42-94783) while 'Special Delivery' was B-24 H-20-FO (42-94896), both flew with the 845th Bomb Squadron.

Close up of 'Special Delivery' after the cockpit armour had been added and ruined the artwork. Much nose art was executed back in the USA when the crews were preparing to leave for England and unaware of the combat modifications their planes would be subject to on arrival. She was eventually transferred to the 445th Bomb Group at Tibenham, while 'Joe' moved to the 453rd Bomb Group.

Ground crew pose by 'Tiger's Revenge' which was later transferred to the 492nd Bomb Group (second organisation) and painted gloss black, but the nose art was preserved. (see also the 492nd Bomb Group section).

Above: B-24 H-1-FO (42-7552) a former 44th Bomb Group machine was used by the 489th Bomb Group. She was known as 'Lil Cookie' and retained the early red outlined national insignia and her original squadron code NB. Yellow polka dots were painted over the original olive-drab.

Below: 489th Bomb Group Liberators form up around 'Lil Cookie' as seen from her left waist window. The nearest plane is 'Ford's Folly' B-24 H-20-FO (42-94824). Inset: The array of signal lights in the modified tail of 'Lil Cookie'.

491st
BOMB GROUP
491st Bombardment
Group (H)

Component Squadrons
Squadron	Code
852nd Sqn	3Q
853rd Sqn	T8
854th Sqn	6X
855th Sqn	V2

Operational base:
Metfield, Suffolk and
North Pickenham,
Norfolk

First mission
2nd June 1944
Last mission
24th April 1945

Group Markings
A white disc containing a dark blue, sometimes black, Z on the upper right wing. Vertical tails were painted green with a white horizontal band.
In Spring 1945 they belatedly repainted their tails in the markings of the former 492nd Bomb Group which they replaced in the 14th Combat Wing. The tails were then silver, with a black diagonal band.
852nd Squadron B-24s had red painted cowl rings. Some silver aircraft grey, or sometimes green, code letters as well as the usual black.

Above and right: **'Little Beaver' B-24 J-150-CO (44-40194)** and **'Johnny Come Lately' B-24 J-140-CO (42-110154)** target bound with the 491st Bomb Group. Both flew with the 855th Bomb Squadron. 'Johnny Come Lately' was one of the very few olive-drab Liberators in the 491st Bomb Group.

Right: **B-24 J-60-CF (44-10534)** from the 852nd Bomb Squadron banks over the Metfield dispersal areas. She was lost on the 26th November 1944 Misburg mission.

Above: A B-24 H-25-FO very soon after being assigned to the 491st Bomb Group. Whilst applying the code letters the painter got his stencils mixed up resulting in this plane carrying 3X instead of 6X. Her career ended on 21st July 1944 during a mission to Kempten, Germany, after a fire in the number 2 engine forced her pilot to land at Dubendorf, Switzerland.

Left: On 20th June 1944 during a mission to a V-Weapons site in northern France an accurate Flak burst blew away the nose turret and the bombardier's station from this 855th Bomb Squadron Lib. Both the navigator and bombardier were killed. The pilot, Lieutenant Stevens, managed to bring this badly crippled B-24 H-25-FO (42-95191) back across the Channel to crash land near Dungeness, Kent, a superb piece of flying.

Left: 'Rage in Heaven' B-24 J-150-CO (44-40165) of the 852nd Bomb Squadron. Later in her career she became the group's second assembly ship.

Above: **A classic portrait of two 855th Bomb Squadron Libs high over the Continent. Nearest is 'Big Un' B-24 J-1-FO (42-50680) whilst coming up in the rear is 'Pegasus'. On the 26th February 1945 Berlin mission the crew had to abandon 'Big Un' over the Russian lines due to severe engine malfunction.**

Left: **Two heavily loaded Liberators flex their wings on the way to their target. Nearest is B-24 J-1-FO (42-50747) and in the background 'Pegasus' B-24 J150-CO (44-40164) once again, both from the 855st Bomb Squadron. The nearest aircraft sports a new, higher profiled, Martin top turret which was introduced on Ford's final Hs and early Js.**

Left: **Could a Liberator have a more apt name? 'Ponderous Pachyderm' B-24 J-145-CO (44-40141) T8-Q of the 853rd Bomb Squadron seen after completing 17 combat missions. She was one of the planes badly damaged when the Metfield bomb dump exploded on 15th July 1944 and was salvaged next day.**

Above: **B-24 J-150-CO (44-40241)** of the 854th Bomb Squadron carried a skull with body, superimposed on a blue disc on her nose and was known as 'The Hard Way'. A circular plate has been riveted over the former ball turret well, many of which were removed from B-24s in the summer of 1944.

Right: Although the 491st Bomb Group transferred from the 95th Combat Bomb Wing to the 14th CBW in the summer of 1944, and technically should have adopted the tail markings of the disbanded 492nd Bomb Group, the group was reluctant to relinquish the green and white tails for the black and white of the 492nd. It did so, all be it belatedly, in the spring of 1945 and consequently few photographs exist of the group's planes in these latter tail feathers. Here two Libs from the 853rd Bomb Squadron release small bombs on the Vomag tank works at Plauen, Germany, on 5th April 1945. Nearest is 'Urgin Virgin' B-24 J-1-FO (42-50754) that survived the war.

Left: 'Ruthless Ruthie' B-24 J-155-CO (44-40317) from the 854th Bomb Squadron. On 16th April 1945, whilst taking off from North Pickenham on a mission to the Landshut marshalling yards, Germany, the left tyre blew. 'Ruthless Ruthie' left the runway at high speed and her right landing gear collapsed, causing her to be written off. The three-piece detachable waist window can be seen leaning against her rear fuselage.

Above and below right: **The 491st Bomb Group had three assembly ships. The first was a veteran from the 389th Bomb Group 'The Little Gramper' B-24 D-90-CO (42-40722), she was painted bright yellow overall and sprinkled with red blotches. That plane was salvaged in August 1944.**

Above: **'Rage in Heaven' B-24 J-150-CO (44-40162) was the second assembly ship and was acquired from the 852nd Bomb Squadron. She flew for a short time with green stripes on her fuselage and wings, but later had the natural metal gaps between the stripes filled with yellow. She crashed in a snow storm when taking off on 5th January 1945.**

Below: **The final 491st assembly ship was 'Tubarao' B-24 J-145-CO (44-40101) from the 854th and later 855th Squadrons, she also carried yellow and green stripes.**

492nd

BOMB GROUP

492nd Bombardment Group (H)

Component Squadrons

Squadron	Code
856th Sqn	5Z
857th Sqn	9H
858th Sqn	9A
859th Sqn	X4

Operational base:
North Pickenham,
Norfolk

First mission
11th May 1944
Last mission
7th August 1944

Group Markings
A white disc containing a dark blue, sometimes black, U on the upper right wing. Discs were painted on the vertical tails of the original planes with the intention of adding the U, but the order was then received to paint a black diagonal band on a white or silver tail.

Above: **B-24 H-25-CF (42-50391) 9A-B of the 858th Bomb Squadron. The Fort Worth assembly plant always painted the olive-drab anti-glare panel all the way forward to the nose turret. 'Old 75' was eventually transferred to the 448th at Seething in June 1944.**

Below: **Two views of B-24 J-55-CF (44-10496) of the 859th Bomb Squadron that staggered into Dubendorf, Switzerland, after sustaining battle damage on the mission to Oberfaffen-hoffen on 21st July 1944. Here the Motor Products A-6-B tail turret is minus its streamlined fairings.**

Above: **San Diego built 'Umbriago' B-24 J-145-CO (44-40068) of the 859th Bomb Squadron braves the Flak in the early summer of 1944.**

When the 492nd arrived in the UK with their mostly silver Liberators in April 1944 they started painting the tails with the Second Bomb Division disc, only to have the markings changed to the black diagonal band in May. In many cases the diagonal band was painted on before the hard pressed ground crews had a chance to remove the disc. As can be imagined, there were always more urgent priorities than painting. When the 492nd Bomb Group disbanded in August 1944 'Umbriago' like many 492nd Liberators transferred to the 467th Bomb Group at Rackheath. Inset: The crew of 'Umbriago' pose before his portrait.

Below: **'Tequila Daisy' was another Lib that limped into Dubendorf, this time on the 11th July 1944 Munich mission. She was B-24 J-150-CO (44-40168) of the 857th Bomb Squadron and had thermal de-icing on all her leading edges.**

Left: 'That's all Brother' B-24 J-145-CO (44-40120) of the 859th Bomb Squadron at the very moment of bomb release, her load is just emerging from the bomb bay in this photo. When the 492nd ceased operations 'That's all Brother' went to the 467th Bomb Squadron at Rackheath. *Inset*: The mission scoreboard on the nose of 'That's all Brother'. She had completed 83 mission at the war's end. This photo reveals many details; the hydraulically operated A-6-B nose turret, armour glass windscreen but not the side windows, armour plate on the cockpit side that appears to have stopped a hit judging by the indentation, flush type pitot tube of the lower fuselage just above and ahead of the nose wheel and inward opening nose wheel doors.

Below: A gleaming, pristine, 'Baby Shoes' B-24 J-1-FO (42-50555) of the 856th Bomb Squadron that later transferred to the 458th Bomb Group at Horsham St Faith.

Below: 'Lucky Lass' B-24 J-15-CO (44-40157) 9H-O of the 857th on her hardstand at North Pickenham. She later went to the 93rd Bomb Group at Hardwick and became a lead ship (see 93rd Bomb Group).

The ill-fated 492nd Bomb Group at North Pickenham used an ex-389th Bomb Group machine, B-24 D-95-CP (42-40743) - see page 21 - as their assembly ship. She had white stripes on her wings, nose and rear fuselage. She retained her mission score board on the extra armour by the pilot's side window, a reminder of her mission to Ploesti on 1st August 1943 indicated by the horizontal bomb.

Below: **A parade at Hethel in the summer of 1944, the 492nd Bomb Group assembly ship can be seen parked near the trees on the right of this picture.**

34th
BOMB GROUP
34th Bombardment Group (H)

Component Squadrons

Squadron	Code
4th Sqn	None
7th Sqn	None
18th Sqn	None
391st Sqn	None

Operational base:
Mendlesham, Suffolk

First mission
23rd May 1944
Last mission
(with B-24s)
24th August 1944

Group Markings
A white square containing a dark blue, sometimes black, S on the outer vertical tails and upper right wing. From late June 1944 the front half of the vertical tails were painted red with the remainder white or silver.

Although squadron codes were not displayed, squadrons were identified by coloured propeller spinners:

White	4th Sqn
Yellow	7th Sqn
Red	18th Sqn
Green	391st Sqn

Above: 'Me, Worry?' B-24 H-20-FO (42-94796) from the 391st Bomb Squadron managed to reach Bulltofta, Sweden, with two damaged engines. She was on the 29th May 1944 mission to Politz.

Below: 'Me, Worry II?' B-24 H-20-FO (42-94942) lost hydraulic brake pressure, but her pilot pulled off a successful landing with the help of parachutes lashed to her waist gun mountings to help slow her down on the runway.

Right: **B-24 H15-FO (42-94787).** Does this name say something about the crew's favourite recreation?

Above: **With her skin glistening in the sunlight 'Betta Duck' cruises over the peaceful Suffolk rural scene in the summer of 1944.**

Right: **'Betta Duck' B-24 J-165-CO (44-40454) displays her novel nose art. She later moved up from Mendlesham to Attlebridge to join the 466th Bomb Group.**

Right: **Walt Disney's cute Fawn 'Bambi' graces the nose of B-24 H-15-CF (41-29567). When the Third Bomb Division changed from 'Libs' to 'Forts' 'Bambi' went to the 458th Bomb Group and became 'My Bunnie'.**

Above: **The twelve man lead crew pose before 'Holy Joe' B-24 J-1-FO (42-50613) . The normal Liberator crew comprised ten men, but H2X or GH leadships needed extra crewmen to man the specialized equipment carried.**

Left: **B-24 J-160-CO (44-40375) displaying her nose art, which is a departure from the usual voluptuous beauty, a gruesome hag riding a bomb. She was transferred to the 445th Bomb Group and survived the war.**

Below: **A practice mission over Suffolk for the 34th Bomb Group. The pastoral panorama below cannot be admired by the pilots and navigators who need to focus all their attention on holding a tight formation and accurate heading.**

486th
BOMB GROUP
486th Bombardment Group (H)

Component Squadrons

Squadron	Code
832nd Sqn	3R
833rd Sqn	4N
834th Sqn	2S
835th Sqn	H8

Operational base:
Sudbury, Suffolk

First mission
7th May 1944
Last mission
(with B-24s)
19th July 1944

Group Markings
A white square containing a dark blue, sometimes black, O on the outer vertical tails and upper right wing.

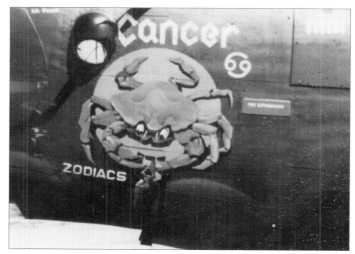

Above: **Scattered cloud over the target as these 486th Libs release their cargo. The silver aircraft is B-24 J-1-FO (42-50561) whilst its companion is 'Cancer' B-24 H-15-FO (42-52650).**

Right: **The nose art of 'Cancer' executed brilliantly by the very talented artist Phil Brinkman, who was responsible for the renditions on all the zodiac squadron's planes and many others.**

Below: **B-24 H-15-FO (42-52765) of the 835th Bomb Squadron came to grief, breaking her back just behind the top turret. Here she is being checked over for re-usable spare parts.**

A further selection of 486th Bomb Group planes carrying Phil Brinkman's superb artwork:
1) 'Aries' B-24 H-15-FO (42-52693)
2) 'Virgo' B-24 H-15-FO (42-52532)
3) 'Libra' B-24 H-15-FO (42-52508)
4) 'Gemini' B-24 H-15-CF (41-29490) Later 'Aries'
5) 'Leo' B-24 H-15-CF (41-29605)
6) 'Hard T'Get' B-24 H-15-FO (42-52753)

487th
BOMB GROUP
487th Bombardment
Group (H)

Component Squadrons

Squadron	Code
836th Sqn	2G
837th Sqn	4F
838th Sqn	2C
839th Sqn	R5

Operational base:
Lavenham, Suffolk

First mission
7th May 1944
Last mission
(with B-24s)
19th July 1944

Group Markings
A white square containing a
dark blue, sometimes black, P
on the outer vertical tails and
upper right wing.

Above and left: **Two photos of B-24 H-15-FO (42-52616) of the 839th Bomb Squadron seen coasting around the perimeter track at Lavenham and at rest on the dispersal area. When the 487th transitioned to B-17s 'Chief Wapello' went to the 44th Bomb Group.**

Left: **A nice piece of artwork on a gleaming B-24 J-155-CO (44-40299). She formerly flew with the 493rd Bomb Group until a crash landing at Woodbridge. After repair she went to the 487th at Lavenham, but eventually found her way out to the Fifteenth Air Force in Italy. On this plane an extra window has been provided for the bombardier and a flush pitot head fitted; all production centres eventually standardised on this type of pitot.**

Above: **The peace at Lavenham is shattered as the 487th Bomb Group prepare for a combat mission. With engines throbbing and brakes squealing the Liberators inch their way to the main runway where they will take off at thirty second intervals. Here again, the de-icer boots have been removed in most cases.**

Three samples of 487th artwork:
'The Spirit of 76' B-24 H-15-FO (42-52776)
'The Tweachewous Wabbit' B-24 H-15-FO (42-52652)
'Solid Sender' B-24 H-15-FO (42-52431)

Component Squadrons

Squadron	Code
848th Sqn	None
849th Sqn	None
850th Sqn	None
851st Sqn	None

Operational base:
Eye, Suffolk

First mission
31st May 1944
Last mission
(with B-24s)
6th August 1944

Group Markings
A white square containing a dark blue, sometimes black, T on the outer vertical tails and upper right wing. From late June 1944 the top third of the vertical tails were painted red with the remainder white or silver.

Above: 'Flying Ginny' B-24 H-20-FO (42-94894) up for a test flight from the air depot at Warton prior to issue to the 490th Bomb Group. She has just been equipped with combat modifications.

Left: 'Flyer's Fancy' B-24 H-20-FO (42-94840) with her recently applied capital T in white square, soon to be re-placed by the white vertical tail with top third painted red. Natural metal leading edges is due to the removal of de-icer boots.

Left: The new red and white tail markings here on B-24 H-15-CF (41-29597) 'Snootie Cutie'.

Below left: 'Snottie Dottie' B-24 H-20-FO (42-94803) of the 851st Bomb Squadron had the heavily armoured pilot's seat, found on B-24Hs, installed. These were known as coffin seats and although affording extra protection were unpopular with most pilots and co-pilots as they were bulky and restricted easy movement.

Below: 'Booby Trap' B-24 H-20-FO (42-94802) of the 850th Bomb Squadron with novel artwork .

493rd

BOMB GROUP
493rd Bombardment Group (H)

Component Squadrons

Squadron	Code
860th Sqn	None
861st Sqn	None
862nd Sqn	None
863rd Sqn	None

Operational base:
Debach, Suffolk

First mission
6th June 1944
Last mission
(with B-24s)
24th August 1944
Total Missions
47

Group Markings

A white square containing a dark blue, sometimes black, X on the outer vertical tails and upper right wing. From late June 1944 the lower portion of the vertical tails were painted red with the remainder white or silver.

The squadrons were also distinguished by coloured propeller bosses:

Squadron	Code
860th Sqn	Yellow
861st Sqn	White
862nd Sqn	Red
863rd Sqn	Blue

Above: **B-24 J-160-CO (44-40357) of the 862nd Bomb Squadron surrounded by her companions. She has yet to reach enemy territory as her waist gun hatches are still closed. When the 493rd converted to B-17s she moved to the 466th Bomb Group at Attlebridge.**

Right: **Forming up over Suffolk farmland with 'Baby Doll' B-24 J-1-FO (42-50554). Ford built Hs and Js carried rubber de-icer boots, but here again these have been removed. It** was Third Division policy to remove them during the warmer summer months. If damaged they could tear loose in the slipstream and jam control surfaces. 'Baby Doll' transferred eventually to the 392nd Bomb Group and survived the war.

Below: **Seen here at Brenzett, Kent, on 31st July 1944 is 'Easy Queen' B-24 J-165-CO of the 862nd Bomb Squadron after a forced landing. Her bomb doors are off their tracks and hanging down. At times these flexible doors would jam only partially open and when the bombs were released they would be torn from their runners. This plane was repaired and transferred to the 466th Bomb Group.**

Above: **A truly terrifying picture of 'Little Warrior' B-24 H-20-FO (42-94812) after she was hit amidships by Flak on the Fellersleben, Germany, mission of 29th June 1944. Fuel lines and oxygen bottles were ruptured with disastrous consequences and in a matter of seconds 'Little Warrior' became an inferno which gave 2nd Lieutenant Hansen's crew no chance of escape.**

Right: **'Ole Baldy' B-24 H-20-FO (42-94863) of the 860th Bomb Squadron. The recently applied navigator's bubble window framing has neatly clipped the right wing of 'Baldy' who went eventually to the 445th Bomb Group at Tibenham.**

Above: **Two views of 'Hairless Joe' B-24 J-160-CO (44-40437) of the 860th Bomb Squadron. The character on the nose was another of Al Capp's creations from the Dogpatch comic strip. She later transferred to the 44th Bomb Group and was damaged beyond repair in a crash landing on 30th November 1944.**

Below: **The B-24's most common ailment was nose wheel failure. This B-24 J-1-FO was a victim on 8th August 1944, but was repaired and eventually transferred to the 392nd at Wendling.**

Above: **B-24 D-1-CO (42-63786)** on the runway at Harrington in the summer of 1944. The 'Carpetbagger's' preferred to use the D version as its glasshouse nose section afforded better visibility for the navigator and nose guns would seldom be practical on night operations.

Above: **Another B-24 D** at its dispersal area with flame dampers on its turbo charger exhausts beneath the nacelles. These created drag, but were absolutely vital on a B-24 at night as the turbos emitted a flame which would be visible for miles.

Left: **A Roman Catholic Mass is being held on the flight line at Harrington, with B-24D 'Midge' as a backdrop.**

801st
BOMB GROUP
801st Bombardment Group (P)
Later 492nd Bomb Group
'The Carpetbaggers'

Component Squadrons

Squadron	Code
36th Sqn	None
406th Sqn	None
788th Sqn	None

Operational bases:
Alconbury, Cambridgeshire
Watton, Norfolk
Harrington, Lincolnshire

First mission
5th April 1944
Last mission
26th April 1945
Total Sorties
2,809

Group Markings
For most of the group's operational career its planes were painted matt black with only top surfaces left olive drab. Late in the war new aircraft were painted gloss black overall with call letters in yellow on the tails.

Above: **Although the B-24D model was favoured by the 'Carpetbaggers', the supply of aircraft was limited and the group had to resort to newer variants such as this B-24H which had its nose turret removed and replaced by a glazed fairing. Also of note on B-24 H-30-DT (42-51211) are the flash eliminators fitted to the tail guns.**

Above: **'Tiger's Revenge' B-24 H-20-FO (42-94816) formerly flew with the 489th Bomb Group and shows the flame dampers well in this view.**

Left: **'Screwball' B-24 H (42-52711) G with the Goldsmith crew. This aircraft has the very high gloss 'anti-searchlight' finish, flash eliminators on the top turret guns, a glazed fairing instead of a nose turret and 'Rebecca' aerial mast just forward of the pitot head mast.**

482nd

BOMB GROUP
482nd Bombardment Group (P) Pathfinder Group

Component Squadrons

Squadron		Code
812th Sqn	B-17s	MI
813rd Sqn	B-17s	PC
814th Sqn	B-24s	SI

Operational bases:
Alconbury, Cambridgeshire

First mission
27th September 1943
Last mission
April 1945

Group Markings
Initially the group received number of B-24s from operational groups and these aircraft operated within the 814th Squadron still in their original markings. Later, new arrivals carried no markings except squadron codes SI on the rear fuselage and a radio call letter on the vertical tails.

Above: B-24 H-1-FO (42-7644) formerly of the 44th Bomb Group, and still carrying that group's markings, leads a formation over Frankfurt on 29th January 1944 and drops 500 pounders with smoke markers. This aircraft is equipped with H2S radar housed in the 'trash can' shaped installation beneath the fuselage. H2S was the forerunner of the improved H2X which later equipped many pathfinder B-24s and B-17s.

Left: **Two views of B-24 M-25-CO (44-42283) with AN/APQ-7 Eagle Radar. Six of these specially equipped Liberators were received by the 482nd Bomb Group and were the only San Diego built Ms to fly with the Eighth Air Force. The machine was operational during the last few days of the air war in Europe. The unique airfoil shaped scanner housing can be seen between the nose wheel and bomb bay. This caused difficulty in flight and landings could be a problem because of the extra lift afforded by what was, in effect, an extra wing.**

803rd
BOMB GROUP

803rd Bombardment Group (P)
Later 36th Bomb Squadron

Component Squadrons

Squadron	Code
36th Sqn	R4

Operational bases:
Oulton, Suffolk
Cheddington,
Buckinghamshire
Alconbury,
Cambridgeshire

First mission
12 July 1944
Last mission
April 1945

Group Markings
Aircraft carried no markings except squadron codes R4 on the rear fuselage and a radio call letter on the vertical tails.

Specialst Task
Jamming enemy radio communications.

Above: **'Lady Jane' B-24 H-25-DT (42-51180) shows her underwing Mandrel and Dina aerials, the transmitters were housed in the bomb bay.**

Right: **Lieutenant Paul Pond and his crew pose by the nose of gloss black Liberator 'Tar Baby' B-24 J-5-DT (42-51311) R4-T.**

Left: **Yet another fearsome face, this time on 'Beast of Bourbon' B-24 H-25-CF (42-50385). 'The Beast' crashed on take-off on 19th February 1945 and was destroyed, the crew members perished.**

Right: The first B-24 model to be equipped with a nose turret was the Ford produced B-24H. This turret was known as the Emerson A-15 and was by far the most efficient type used. Unfortunately production of the turret did not keep pace with the production of Liberators, leading to use of other lesser turrets. When production of Emersons increased it became the standard turret of late-war Liberators. The Emerson was electrically controlled, roomier that other turrets, and had good visibility. This photo was taken at the huge Ford complex at Willow Run, Michigan and shows the gun barrels taped over for transit.

NOSE TURRETS

Right: Early San Diego and Fort Worth J models reaching the Eighth Air Force were initially furnished with the Consolidated A-6-A turret in the nose. This was actually the original Liberator rear turret with extra fairings to improve airflow and reduce draughts and drag. It was hydraulically operated and the guns were staggered with the left weapon protruding further than the right.

Right: The Motor Products Company produced a turret which was an improvement on the basic Consolidated design. This was known as the MPC A-6-B and offered improved side visibility, aligned guns and a curved sighting glass instead of the original flat glass. Consolidated at San Diego produced most of its Js with this turret until late in the production run, whilst it became standard in the tail of most Liberators. In this view the turret is fitted to B-24 J-145-CO (44-40100) 3Q-E of the 491st Bomb Group.

TAIL AND BALL TURRETS

Above: **Initially the turrets on Eighth Air Force B-24s were the Consolidated A-6-A model, seen here on a 453rd Bomb Group B-24H. This turret featured staggered guns and was used on B-24 Ds, early Hs and early Js.**

Above right: **The Motor Products Company improved the design which was used on late Hs, late Js and M models.**

Right: **B-24 Ls arriving in the UK late in 1944 had a novel light-weight tail gun position which saved weight and shortened the rear fuselage. In this installation the guns were closer together and hand operated.**

Left: **The Briggs/Sperry ventral ball-turret was used on late production B-24 Ds and also Hs and Js until the early summer of 1944 when they were removed from Eighth Air Force B-24s. Some Bomb Group commanders considered it prudent to cover vulnerable positions in the formation and a few B-24s retained the ball-turrets until the very end of the war.**

Right: **The standard top turret on early machines operating with the Eighth Air Force was the Martin A-3-B, seen here on 'Liberty Lad' a B-24D of the 93rd Bomb Group in late 1942. the gunner is T/Sgt Al Lee.**

Lower right: **Mid-way through 1944 new B-24s arriving in the United Kingdom were sporting an updated version of the Martin turret, known as the A-3-D. This had a higher profile allowing extra head room for the gunner when the guns were in the depressed position. It was unofficially known as the 'high-hat' turret and featured on late model Hs, Js, Ls and Ms.**

TOP TURRETS AND WAIST GUN WINDOWS

Below: **Waist-gun positions were originally hatches hinged at the top and opening inwards and upwards. A slipstream deflector in front of the hatch helped slightly to protect the hapless gunner from the sub-zero gale. Here Sergeant De Sales Glover poses at his position. After six missions with the 458th Bomb Group he was found to be only 16 years old, having given a false age when he enlisted at just 14!**

Below right: **Enclosed, fully glazed, waist windows were introduced in the spring of 1944 on 'Batch 20' of the Ford and Fort Worth built B-24Hs. The gun was now mounted in a swivel below the window, known as the K-6 gun mount. Later models had an extended glazed area further down the fuselage and incorporated the gun mount in the window itself.**

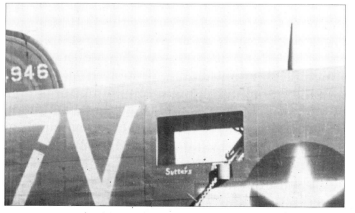

Formation Assembly Ships

To the citizens of East Anglia, who by 1944 had become rather blasé concerning the wide variety of British and American aircraft constantly above their heads, the occasional appearance of weird looking Liberators painted in the most outrageous, garish, colours and patterns gave rise to an amount of speculation. To see colourful nose art, usually in the form of voluptuous females was quite normal; but this seemed crazy. Had the mad bloody Yanks taken leave of their senses? The reason for this apparent madness was far from light hearted.

As the year of 1944 progressed with ever more B-24 Groups becoming operational and increasing numbers of bombers setting out on almost daily bombing missions, the problems of formation assembly had become more and more evident. Usually bombing missions were initiated at first light and entailed hundreds of B-24s, taking off at 30 second intervals, from over a dozen bases and climbing up and circling to form their combat group formations. Within a very short period of time the restricted air space above East Anglia would be, seemingly, crowded with heavy bombers circling in the murk. This take off and assembly procedure could be an ordeal for the combat crews involved and many considered it as hazardous as combat itself. Taking a heavily overloaded B-24, pregnant with explosive ordnance and fuel, into the air and needing every foot of runway was ordeal enough; the next problem was to coax the roaring, lurching, unstable monster to the assembly area through several thousand feet of turbulent cloud. On most occasions visibility would be minimal with the added hazards of invisible prop-wash from other aircraft plus, maybe, icing conditions – probably the aviator's worst enemy. Ice could, within a few seconds, turn a windscreen opaque, it could distort and spoil the aerodynamic shape of the wings and tailplane, lock the control surfaces and block air intakes.

Whilst trying to cope with all these problems the pilots had to fly the most accurate compass course possible as a slight deviation could take the aircraft into another group's airspace with the possibility of collision. Once assembly altitude had been reached the next problem for the pilot was trying to distinguish his own bomb group from among the myriad of circling Libs. Visibility was often minimal and even if the clouds had been topped, the low sun caused excessive glare.

These hazards had to be faced day after day and the Eighth Air Force badly needed to solve the problem of group identification. Initially, during the late Summer of 1943, it was decided that each group should carry an individual letter within a large white disc on the vertical tails, in the Third Division a white square was used. As more groups became operational it was admitted that this method still failed to solve the problem and in May 1944 the discs gave way to distinctive coloured vertical tails with bisecting black or white bands either vertical, diagonal or horizontal. This method improved the situation somewhat, but these colours were still hard to distinguish in the early morning light.

It was then decided that a single brightly and individually painted B-24 taking off ahead of its parent bomb group and circling in the assembly area whilst firing flares and flashing the individual group letter might help the situation. There were several war weary aircraft in the various groups, usually old D versions, which were ideal for this job and these were farmed out to the combat units for conversion. In most cases, but not all, excess weight such as armament and armour plate was removed. The aircraft were then fitted with signal lights that could be seen from a great distance and then painted in the brightest and most distinctive colours that would be discernable in the most adverse conditions. These planes became known as 'assembly ships' or 'Judas goats' and, although they did not solve all the problems of group, wing and division assembly, they helped enormously.

In spite of all the amused head shaking of the East Anglian locals, it had to be admitted that there was method in the 'daft bloody Yanks' madness after all.

Just returned from her assembly duties on a warm summer's day at Horsham St Faith 'Spotted Ape' (41-28697) eases her weary bones onto her hardstand. She formerly flew missions with the group as 'Dixie Belle 2nd'.